101 WAYS TO
simplify your life

101 WAYS TO
simplify your life

HOW TO
DECLUTTER
YOUR MIND,
BODY, AND
SOUL

suzannah
olivier

CICO BOOKS

London

First published in 2003 by Cico Books Ltd
32 Great Sutton Street London EC1V 0NB

10 9 8 7 6 5 4 3 2 1

A CIP catalogue record for this book is available from the
British Library

ISBN 1 903116 42 2

Photographs © Cico Books page: 12, 14, 32, 34, 45
            © Cico Books/Gloria Nicol page: 91
            © Cico Books/Simon Brown page: 56, 58, 59,
            64, 67, 68, 81
            © Sarah Cuttle/Mainstream page 46, 28; Ray
Main/Mainstream pages 1,3, 18, 20, 25, 42, 61, 62, 70, 73,
74, 85, 88, 92; Ray Main/Mainstream/David Gill page 54;
Ray Main/Mainstream/Designer Claire Nash page 5; Ray
Main/Mainstream/Designer Nick Monroe page 70

Edited by Alison Wormleighton
Designed by Christine Wood
Artworks by Anthony Duke

Printed and bound in Singapore

Note: Please be aware that the information contained in
this book and the opinions of the author are not a
substitute for medical attention and treatment. If you are
worried about any aspect of your health, ask a medical
professional before proceeding. The publishers and author
can take no responsibility for any injury or illness resulting
from the advice given in this book. For safety reasons, never
use essential oils undiluted.

Contents

it can be so simple

It's time to untangle your overcomplicated life and restore harmony. This book shows you how to unlearn bad habits, declutter your home and lifestyle, and restore simple pleasures. A healthy, stress-free life is yours for the taking.

Simplifying your life is not about giving yourself more to do. If you look at this book and immediately see an ever-lengthening list of extra things to do in order to find simplicity, you are missing the main message. This book shows you how to find space in your life and to pare situations down to their basic components. Finding solutions that work means finding the easiest route to a pleasing answer.

There is also an instinctive aspect to simplifying your life. We have lost touch with our environment and our true nature. Frequently we deal with problems by anesthetizing ourselves. Sticking our head in the sand, worrying about a situation, or just drowning our sorrows really doesn't work. In the long term, these behavior patterns only defer the moment of truth, or, even worse, create further problems to deal with. In such ways, we make simple situations complicated. Becoming more in tune to our needs and more instinctive about what works helps to simplify life.

We live in a complicated world – things to do, obligations to meet, as well as information overload and all sorts of personal anxieties about our ability to deal with these. We can get into the habit of being busy and putting up with its attendant complications. Sometimes a mass of things to do becomes our solution to space and silence that we are not used to. It is as if we need to fill what we perceive as voids in life. But we need to learn to embrace space and silence for real equilibrium. Our reactions to given situations are usually a result of years of learned behavior and thought patterns. You may not even realize what your automatic

reactions are. By giving yourself the time to study these reactions and by adopting new patterns that serve you better, you begin to find harmony, to court simplicity and to do instinctively what is best for you, your family, and friends.

You can start a chain reaction. Once you are working positively on one area of your life, you start to feel good about yourself and about what you are doing. Each section in this book covers a major area of life. You'll find highly practical solutions to common problems, including many quick fixes, as well as tips on how to promote health and nurture relationships. And although the main areas are looked at separately, the book takes a holistic approach, creating solutions that enhance and strengthen each other. Learning to simplify your day will help you make the most of your life.

time to
take action

How did life get complicated? This is a question we all ask ourselves from time to time. It can seem as if life sneaks up and overwhelms us. It's time to take action.

These are some of the major areas for complications in life – identify which of them are most relevant to your life.

1 TOO MUCH TO DO

This can be brought about because:

● You don't know how to say no and so you end up amassing obligations.

● You are unrealistic about the time various tasks take. The solution is to think about what you are taking on. Do a time audit for a couple of days and see how you really spend your time. If you are asked to do something and an outright "no" is difficult, say you'll think about it. You can then either say no or add your conditions to make it feasible.

2 BACKLOG OF THINGS TO DO

A sure sign of this is if:

● Your home or desk is a junkyard.

● You procrastinate about things and they build up. The solution is to streamline your life. Become ruthless about getting rid of unnecessary items. Procrastination can be a sign that we are not enjoying the job. We are less likely to procrastinate about doing things we enjoy, so do more of what you like doing. Delegate or hire help when you need to.

3 INABILITY TO MAKE DECISIONS

When you delay decisions, the problems take on a life of their own and become even bigger. Your decision-making ability needs work if:

● Problems are keeping you awake at night.

● You want to please everyone and end up pleasing no one. The solution is to take action, no matter how small, and you will make future choices less painful. Don't worry about making the wrong decision. If worst comes to worst, you will learn from your mistakes. But the chances are that if you take action more often, you will instinctively become better at making decisions.

4 FINANCIAL MESS

Money, or the lack of it, is often at the root of complications and dissent. You know you need to act if:

● You would rather not open your bank or credit card statements.

● You often worry about how your finances are going to work out.

● You are a binge spender, believing that tomorrow will take care of itself.

The solution is to get on top of the problem once and for all. Make a finite list of your expenses and your income and see where the shortfalls happen. If necessary, refinance your debts, and start afresh. Make a payment schedule and stick to it while cutting back on your spending.

5 TENDENCY TO INVITE COMPLICATIONS OR DISASTERS

Have you noticed how some people always seem to invite trouble? Symptoms are:

● A tendency to see things in a gloomy way.

● Avoiding taking action instead of dealing with the root cause of a problem, which only leads to the problem worsening and others developing.

The solution is to lighten up. A problem is just a challenge and there will always be a solution of some sort, even if it is not ideal. By worrying, you don't actually resolve it.

6 POOR COMMUNICATION

Good communication is an art, and complications often happen when it is not applied. Signs of communication problems are:

● Jumping in with both feet and assuming that others see situations in the same way as you do.

● Not getting the results you'd like from many situations.

Try to listen to other people first to get their point of view before letting them know what your needs are. It helps if you can always be truthful about your viewpoint, to avoid creating a stance for yourself that is difficult to retreat from.

your
MIND

10-second
stress-reducers

How exactly do you reduce stress in 10 seconds? To do so may seem impossible – after all, you might not be able to change whatever has brought the stress on in the first place. And when you are in the midst of feeling bad about something, turning it around in such a short time might seem to be expecting too much.

But it can be done. The trick is to change your state of mind, your attitude, or your viewpoint. By changing how you feel about something, in an instant you can feel better. We very often do this quite naturally. For instance, if you are feeling sorry for yourself and then something bad happens elsewhere, your own woes are instantly brought into perspective. Similarly, when you are having a row with someone and suddenly something funny happens and you both dissolve into laughter, all at once things don't seem so bad – and you are friends again.

Knowing that 10-second stress-reducers can be used all the time is helpful for the next step. You now need to harness this phenomenon to enable you to bring it into play whenever you wish. It takes practice, mainly to remind yourself to take action when appropriate, but the rewards can be instantaneous.

● Don't dwell on the bad times for too long. Get into the habit of focusing on the good times instead. If you catch yourself feeling bad about something, change your mood by thinking about things that excite you. Right now jot down three things that delight and inspire you.

● Feeling bored, lonely, or sad? Pick up the phone and make an arrangement for some time in the near future to do something you can look forward to. You are not creating an instant activity, but by taking positive action – even if you just leave a message on a friend's answering machine about

> We overestimate what we can achieve in a day, but underestimate what we can accomplish in a month.

going to the movies, or book yourself on a weekend course – you are giving yourself something to look forward to.

● Laughter really is the best medicine. Indulge in "laughter therapy" when you feel stressed – no matter what others think of you, laugh it off. If you are tired after a long day, watch a comedy show rather than the news on TV; the laughter will relax you, whereas the news may not.

● If you feel the adrenaline rising in any given situation, adopt a deep-breathing technique (don't do this if you are hyperventilating with a panic attack). Stop what you are doing for a moment, still yourself, and breathe deeply in through your nose for a count of five, expanding your lungs from the bottom upward. Do not hold your breath, but breathe out slowly through your mouth for a count of 10, squeezing the last drop of breath out of your lungs. All the while say to yourself, "I am calm." Repeat five times.

● Take pleasure in small, repetitive tasks instead of getting annoyed by them. The Zen Buddhist approach is, "If enlightenment happens as a result of chopping wood, keep chopping wood."

● Don't let trivia bother you. Recognize that in life in general, we all focus too much on trivia.

STRESS-FREE LIVING POINTS 1–5

○ If you are stuck in heavy traffic…
Think: What's the hurry? I'm enjoying the journey.

○ If you've just been denied a promotion. Think: I have an incentive to explore other employment opportunities.

○ If you've broken up with your lover…
We had a good time, but now that I have only myself to think of, I am going to do exactly as I please.

○ If you've received bad news…
Think: What can I do right now that is positive and that will improve the situation?

○ The more often you take positive action, the more of a habit it will become. Soon you will virtually have wiped the words "bored," "lonely," and "sad" from your vocabulary.

simple mind tricks to
stay calm

There are plenty of ways to get a head start on serenity; the most effective result from focusing outside yourself:

● Be nice to others. It's not hard – it just takes practice. If you doubt the value of simply being nice, listen to this story. One company has recently increased its profits by 200 percent simply by introducing a policy of being nice to its staff. Employees get a hug from their boss each morning, the company sponsors social evenings every two weeks, music is played in the office, and there is a ban on overtime. No one argues in the office anymore, it is a relaxed place to work, and the increase in profits speaks for itself.

● Learn something new. Perhaps it will be something that excites you or has drawn you for a while though you've done nothing about it until now. Learning new skills can boost your confidence and get you away from behavior patterns that do not serve you well. It can change your social life and give you something to look forward to at the end of the day or week. It might even be a life-changing experience. The ideal is to have a range of activities – some to challenge you physically or mentally enough to tire you out in a healthy way, some for socializing, and some for solitary time.

● Feed your mind with beauty and learning: visit an art gallery; lie down and listen to classical music; study a flower; read or, even better, learn a poem.

● Stop labeling yourself. It may seem comforting to identify why you have a problem, but the flip side to this coin is that you begin to live the life of the label "I am a depressive," "I have an addictive personality," "I have low self-esteem," and so on. In today's society all the seven deadly sins have become behavior problems that require treatment. Shed the label and you have a better chance of shedding the behavior pattern.

relax... and keep your edge

You might be proud of the fact that you live life at full throttle, believing that the adrenaline rush you get keeps you alert and focused. Yet this common addiction to the pressure-fix misses an important point: being serene does not mean losing your "edge."

There is nothing to stop you from being calm, serene, and tuned in while leading a busy life. Redirect your energy, for just five minutes, from the immediate problem and you will feel refreshed and capable.

SIGHT – This is a new version of I-Spy. Take a walk, or just sit at your desk, and pick something to focus on. Look for unusually shaped clouds; or count how many people are wearing something red, how many unusual buildings you see, or how many people look happy or sad.

SMELL – Smells are highly evocative and, in an instant, can transport you back to familiar, happy memories. Concentrate on recalling the smells of happy times. Flower scents give an instant uplift, so enjoy these in the form of aromatherapy oils, such as geranium or rose. Use lavender, which can be used undiluted, or other essences diluted in a ratio of 1–3 percent essential oil to 97–99 percent base oil such as almond or avocado.

TASTE – Take time in order to savor your food. Eat it much more slowly than you normally would, rolling the taste around in your mouth and enjoying all the flavors. The mouth and lips have the highest concentrations of nerve endings, so let your taste buds take over… and banish those extraneous thoughts.

HEARING – Instead of being aware of the chatter in your head and in the immediate vicinity, focus on noises outside the room you are in. Mentally extend your aural senses and listen to the sounds of traffic and birds outside, distant voices, or a bee or bug buzzing by.

TOUCH – Sit in a chair for five minutes. Close your eyes and become conscious of the sensations of your body. Start to feel the pressure of your legs and back on your chair: hold an object in your hand, and for several minutes remain aware of the sensations of touching this object.

mind yoga

Yoga is a powerful, and yet so simple, workout for the mind as well as for the body. It is an opportunity, for relatively little input, to develop suppleness and to reach peak physical condition, but it is also a time for silence that soothes the mind.

There is no competition in yoga. You go completely at your own pace and must not strain. You can start each pose at your own level and very slowly increase the stretch over time to a point that is completely comfortable for you. By focusing on the position and on your breathing, you give your mind a real vacation.

Choose a place where you will not be disturbed and which is at a comfortable temperature, and do the exercises on a carpet or a yoga mat. Wear loose-fitting, comfortable clothing.

During the pose, breathe naturally, through your nose, concentrating on even breathing. Hold the positions for 10–20 seconds, breathing all the time. Soften your gaze and quiet your hearing. Keep your face and jaw muscles relaxed. Come out of the poses the way you went into them (i.e. return to standing, lying, kneeling, or another position). All one-sided positions must subsequently be reversed and done on the other side. Work through all the positions once, then repeat the individual positions as many times as you like.

STRESS-FREE LIVING POINTS 6–10

❍ Do a 15-minute session of yogic breathing, known as pranayama, for an instant energy boost and de-stress. Beginners should practice the exercises lying flat, their spine supported by a bolster or rolled blanket, relaxing in the resting pose (see page 17). As you progress you will be able to move to a sitting position and you can even practice while at work.

❍ Take up your position and relax, just concentrating on the flow of your breathing. Notice its uneven patterns – when you even out and calm your breathing, you will calm your mind.

❍ Now focus on the in-breath, breathing in through your nose and keeping the breath slow and smooth.

❍ Breathe out through your mouth, in the same slow way, and repeat. Make sure your face and shoulder muscles are relaxed, and observe the gentle rise and fall of the abdomen as you breathe.

❍ Continue "shaping" your breathing in this way for 10–15 minutes. Rest for a few seconds before continuing your day revived and reinvigorated.

COBRA STRETCH

1 Lying on your stomach, place your hands flat on the floor with your thumbs level with your armpits.

2 As you breathe out, raise your head slowly and arch your back. Keep your lower body as still as you can. Your chest should feel as if it is opening up and your spine lengthening. Do not hunch your shoulders.

3 Increase the stretch as far as is comfortable into the full cobra stretch. Keep the movement slow and controlled, and hold the position before lowering yourself slowly back down to the floor.

BALANCE POSTURE

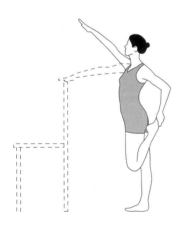

1 You might need to hold the back of a chair initially to achieve the basic position, shown above. When you are ready, let go of the chair, and keep your arm raised.

2 When you have mastered the basic position, bring the forward arm down slowly until it is parallel with the floor and extend the leg that you are holding at the back. Hold the position.

3 Now straighten up to the basic position again. Repeat on the other side of the body.

DOWNWARD DOG

1 Start on all fours with your knees directly under your hips and the heels of your hands beneath your shoulders.

2 Keeping your hands still, lift your hips until your legs are straight.

3 Press your heels into the floor. Lower your head between your arms and push the floor away with your hands. Hold and then return to the kneeling position on all fours.

TREE POSE

1 Stand straight, with your toes to the front, your weight evenly distributed, the spine elongated, your chin parallel to the floor, and shoulders relaxed.

2 Shift your weight onto one foot, feeling as though you are rooted through your spread foot into the floor. Draw your other foot up and place it as high as is comfortable on the other leg, with the toes aimed downward toward the floor and the knee drawn out as close to a right angle as you can.

3 Lift your arms over your head keeping your shoulders loose. Extend your fingers toward the ceiling and keep your arms parallel with your ears. Press your foot and opposite thigh firmly into each other, keeping your hips square. Take your tailbone down to elongate your lower spine. Hold and then return to standing.

CHILD POSE

1 Kneel on the floor, feet together. Sit on your heels, then separate your knees to hip width (keeping your toes together). If you have difficulty sitting on your heels, place a thickly folded blanket between the back of your thighs and calves.

2 Lay your upper body between your thighs. Lengthen your tailbone and your skull away from the back of your neck.

3 Lay your hands on the floor alongside your torso, palms up. Feel the weight of the front of your shoulders open up your shoulder blades across your back.

RESTING POSE

1 This pose helps put your body into a neutral position – an essential skill in yoga. It is the pose that is used at the end of all yoga sessions – aim to do it for five minutes for each 30 minutes of yoga. Sit on the floor with your knees bent.

2 Lower your upper body to the floor by leaning on your elbows first. Release both legs, flatten the groin, and turn both feet out evenly. Lift the base of your skull away from the back of the neck and position comfortably. Reach your arms toward the ceiling, rock slightly from side to side to broaden the back, and release your arms to the floor.

3 Relax all the major muscle groups, then concentrate on the tiny muscles. Relax the muscles in your ankles, wrists, jaw, forehead, at the back of your skull, and at the back of your tongue and palate.

meditation

Meditation is a way of stilling the mind in a frantic world. Bringing mental calm into your life will help you take a more creative approach to your life, with a calmer mind. You will create the opportunity to reflect on the next step, and feel both invigorated and more relaxed. A number of physical health problems can be improved by meditation, including irritable bowel syndrome, chronic pain, and fatigue.

Tension, anxiety, stress, and depression are increasing problems. While there are many tools for dealing with these, from counseling, to exercise, to medication, all also respond well to relaxation and calming therapy. Meditation is an ideal way to improve your ability to overcome these challenges. You can meditate at any time you like. You do not need special equipment, a special place, or a large amount of time. It is not essential to sit cross-legged in a darkened room. Instead, wherever you are, notice such things as the shape of a leaf, the changing colors of the sky at dusk, or how long it takes an ant to scurry across your path. All this is meditation. Some goal-oriented people find it hard to understand that the meditation destination is not a fixed point. Rather, the destination is actually the process, or the "journey." Instead of trying to control the situation, just let it happen.

MINDFULNESS

Mindfulness is a practical, everyday form of meditation. To be mindful, devote 30 minutes during the day when you concentrate fully on savoring a particular task or activity, preferably one that is low-key. You could be cooking the evening meal, you could be sewing something, you could be washing your hair. Take the phone off the hook at this time. When concentrating on mindfulness you devote your full attention to the task, without being distracted, so that you really relish the activity. Repetitive tasks are particularly good for mindfulness. For instance, when you are chopping an apple, examine the fruit and become very aware of its smell, color, texture, and shape. As you chop it, notice the change in aroma and the feel of the cut flesh. Notice when the flesh of the apple changes color. Taste a little piece and roll it around your mouth. Notice the taste sensation as you hold the apple in your mouth. Now bite into it and notice the change in taste. Slowing yourself down in this way is extremely calming.

STRESS-FREE LIVING POINTS 11–17

○ Meditation is an effective and increasingly popular way to de-stress. As you practice, the benefits improve. Sit in a comfortable position preferably in a quiet room at a comfortable temperature.

○ Close your eyes or focus on an object, such as the flickering flame of a candle.

○ Focus on your breathing and become aware of your in and out breaths. Breathe in through your nose and out through your mouth.

○ Relax your shoulders and your face, neck, and jaw muscles and become more relaxed overall.

○ Choose a mantra that is meaningful to you. A mantra is a soothing word or sound that helps to focus your attention and prevent you from getting distracted. Repeat it in a low, rhythmic voice, or if you prefer, just think the mantra. Instead of a mantra you could choose a positive affirmation or a visualization.

○ If thoughts come into your mind, recognize them as simply thoughts, rather than allowing yourself to become distracted by them. You can't stop thoughts happening, but you can view them in an abstract way and put a distance between yourself and your mind. Instead of interacting with them, observe your thoughts.

○ Meditate for at least 10 minutes, or for 15–20 minutes if you are able to, each day.

aromatherapy
for relaxation

Aromatherapy is one of the oldest therapies still practiced today, having been used by ancient cultures such as the Egyptians, the Greeks, and the Romans. Aromatherapy oils and massage can encourage the mind and body to relax, harmonize, and find well-being. For instance, research has shown that when commuters are surrounded by calming scents, such as lavender, which promotes brain waves associated with relaxation, their aggressive behavior is reduced by nearly half.

Aromatherapy oils are concentrated essences of plants. You can buy individual oils or ready-made formulas. Oils can be used for massage, to add to baths, or to put into a diffuser that releases scent into a room. They are also incorporated into candles. You can rub a drop or two of a calming oil blend, such as lavender, into your temples or your chest or put drops on a handkerchief.

RELAXING BATH SOAK

To unwind at the end of the day, indulge in a warm to hot bath to which you have added four to six drops of relaxing essences. After your bath, wrap yourself in a warm, soft towel and relax. Sip a calming herb tea such as mint, melissa, or vervain. Relaxing oils to use in your bath could be a mixture of two or three of the following: lavender, ylang-ylang, basil, marjoram, melissa, neroli, petitgrain, clary sage, orange, or mandarin.

REFRESHING BATH SOAK

When your energy is flagging and you want to revive yourself, perhaps before an evening out, add lemon, grapefruit, or bergamot oil to the bathwater. It is also invigorating to take a brisk shower, in which case rub in some of the oil afterward for a similar effect.

CALMING MASSAGE OIL

As a base oil for massage, use a light oil such as sweet almond or cold-pressed sunflower oil. For a richer base oil that will serve as a nourishing skin food, use avocado or wheatgerm. Add six to 10 drops of aromatherapy oil to five teaspoons of base oil. Make up a mixture of lavender and sandalwood in base oil to use whenever you need it. Never use essential oils undiluted.

WARMING MUSCLE RUB

To ease tired muscles, perhaps after traveling a long distance, or after a vigorous workout, add rosemary, black pepper, and lemongrass to a base oil. Warm it in your hands before massaging with long, smooth strokes.

MIND-FOCUS VAPORIZER BLEND

Keep a vaporizer on your desk and add eucalyptus and basil oil when you find that your mind is wandering or you are tired yet need to concentrate.

HORMONAL HELPERS

To perk yourself up if you are feeling low because of premenstrual hormone troubles, chamomile, geranium, cypress, or clary sage oil can work magic. A warm bath with parsley, neroli, or pine oil added to the water is also a help. Massage diluted parsley or neroli oil into your abdomen. Drink chamomile tea to reduce water retention.

MOOD ENHANCERS

Plants and plant oils have an effect on the nervous system and can help lift your spirits when you are depressed. If you are feeling tearful, unmotivated, or despondent, herb oils such as marjoram, thyme, neroli, basil, and verbena are effective. Mix a few drops of any of these oils with grape-seed oil and use it in the bath. To help you feel centered, rub the mix into your solar plexus, just above your navel.

20 calming foods

It is no secret that certain moods can send us straight to our favorite comfort food or tipple. But what is less well known is that our food choices also influence how we feel. What we eat can have a positive influence on our moods and behavior. Unfortunately, we can become attached to the behavior and eating patterns that serve us least well. By taking a different approach, and consciously incorporating more food and drink choices that improve the situation, you will start to feel calmer and more in control. It's not just foods themselves that have a calming effect – the way you eat them also does. Even if your day is action-packed, enjoy leisurely mealtimes in order to get maximum benefit from your food.

1 Include protein foods, such as legumes (including peas, beans, lentils, soybeans, and alfalfa), nuts, fish, meat, and cheese in your meals. Protein foods are sources of tryptophan, a calming brain chemical. If you are prone to mood swings, eating a little protein with each meal can help.

2 Oats are the classic relaxation food and have been used by herbalists for centuries as a calming remedy. As a whole grain they also help to balance blood sugar. In addition, oats, like other carbohydrates, help the brain to process tryptophan.

3 Milk is rich in calcium, though the mineral is better absorbed from skim milk than from whole milk. Calcium's calming properties have led to the use of warm milk as a nightcap. However, mature cheeses cannot be used in a similar way. Though these have lots of calcium, they also contain tyramine, which can sometimes induce migraines and nightmares.

4 If you are dairy-intolerant, enjoy a nightcap made of calcium-enriched soya milk or rice milk.

5 Familiar in Italian cooking, basil is a highly calming food and can help to induce sleepiness. It is easy to keep a plant pot handy to snip leaves into salads. Pesto sauce, made from fresh basil, will give a strong sleep-inducing boost, while tomato and basil salads and soups are delicious.

6 Calming herb teas, or tisanes, are good to drink instead of coffee, which can make you jittery. Some soothing options include chamomile, lemon balm, and lavender – drink them individually or blend two together.

7 Molasses is the sweet residue left behind after sugar is refined. Because too much sugar can aggravate blood-sugar swings, and so worsen moods, you could consider using molasses as a substitute. Molasses is high in minerals, including calcium and magnesium, that balance the nervous system. It has a strong flavor, so use only a small amount.

8 Other sugar substitutes include a little unrefined honey (manuka honey is highest in compounds that fight infections), dried fruit (high in magnesium and iron), sweet fruits such as bananas (high in nerve-balancing potassium), and FOS (fructo-oligosaccharides), a sprinkle sweetener/fiber that keeps bowels healthy.

9 It is thought that the reason chocolate makes us feel better is that it triggers the same brain chemicals that are released when we are in love. Eat a modest amount of high-quality chocolate (one with 60–70 percent cocoa solids is ideal).

STRESS-FREE LIVING POINTS 18–21

○ Plan your meals in advance so when you are tired or busy you don't wind up gobbling down whatever is most convenient but may be least nutritious.

○ At every opportunity, set the table or make your plate of food beautifully presented and appealing – we eat with our eyes as well as our mouth.

○ Consciously make time for meals instead of eating on the run. Even 15 minutes of relaxed dining in peaceful surroundings will make a difference.

○ Give yourself time to digest your food. Rush and stress literally shut down the digestive tract and impair digestion. Instead of racing off as soon as you put your fork down, choose a quieter and more relaxed activity for a while.

10 You may think that alcohol calms you down, but it actually deadens feelings if you overdo it. To maintain your vitality, choose orange juice with sparkling water, tonic water with Angostura bitters, or a tomato and celery Virgin Mary juice.

11 Selenium is great for maintaining mood balance. Brazil nuts are rich in this mineral and three or four a day will give you enough, as well as providing a handy snack. Other selenium-rich foods include rice, wheat, seaweed, and seafood, especially shrimp and tuna.

12 Oily fish are rich in omega-3 essential fats. One of these fats, DHA, is found in the brain in large quantities (the brain is 60 percent fat and the makeup of these fats is important). Fish oils have been shown to alleviate depression and hyperactivity.

13 Magnesium-rich foods are vital to help calm the mind and balance moods, particularly if you are prone to PMS (premenstrual syndrome). Green leafy vegetables are rich in magnesium; other sources include dried fruit, nuts, seeds, and legumes. For a magnesium boost, add some green leafy vegetables, such as dark green cabbage leaves, to your daily vegetable juice.

14 Pear, celery, and ginger juice is delicious and a good mood booster. Pear is rich in potassium for brain function, celery is used by herbalists as a nerve tonic, and ginger peps you up. Put one pear, one or two celery sticks, and a 1-inch (2.5cm) cube of root ginger in a juicer, and liquidize till smooth.

15 Selected herbs steeped in boiling water for 10 minutes provide a useful antidote for tension headaches. For two cups, use 1½ teaspoons of mixed dried skullcap (a mild sedative), lavender flowers (soothing), and lemon verbena (calming). Strain and sweeten the mixture with a little honey.

16 The B-vitamins and vitamin C are important anti-stress nutrients that help calm the nervous system. Try tangerine and raspberry juice, or carrot, beansprout, and cranberry juice.

17 Lettuce-based juices are excellent for helping you relax at bedtime. Lettuce has a strong flavor, so mix it with carrot juice.

18 All fruits and vegetables are rich in antioxidants. Along with their other benefits (anti-cancer, anti-heart disease), antioxidants help prevent age-related brain degeneration. Fruit and vegetables are also our main source of potassium, an important mineral for soothing the nerves. Eat five portions of fresh fruit and vegetables daily.

19 Mint is a herb that helps lower feelings of anger and nervousness, especially "butterflies in the stomach." Add it liberally to salads or sprinkle it on vegetables. Mint tea makes a soothing drink.

20 Zinc and iron are essential for optimum brain function, mental health, and mood balance. Good sources of these minerals include lean meats, seafood, nuts, seeds, whole grains, and legumes such as peas, beans, lentils, soybeans, and alfalfa.

become an expert on you

Your individual beliefs affect the choices you make in all aspects of your life: work, leisure, and relationships. Your mind-set, or belief system, governs how you live your life, react to circumstances, and communicate with other people. For example, when you get upset or are frustrated by a situation, it is always because your rules for living have been transgressed in some way. Changing the rules you have set for your life, if you think it is appropriate, is the way to reduce the number of times you get upset or frustrated.

Understanding your beliefs, what has shaped you, how you respond to experiences, and what your priorities are can help you to be happier and to shape your future according to your own aims.

We all need to learn lessons from our experiences – this may seem obvious but it does not always happen, which is why we repeat patterns of behavior and can feel as if we are going around in circles. If you are determined to learn from each situation, you also create an environment where you always win: either you achieve what you desire, or you learn sufficiently from the experience to make a more educated stab at achieving it later. And while it is useful to evaluate and learn from past experiences, it is not a good idea to live in the past. It is more constructive to live for the present and to be excited about the future.

A recent large-scale wellbeing survey found that there were five key "drivers" of wellbeing and 10 further drivers of it. These are listed below in the order of importance identified in the survey. See how you score on each of them, to evaluate what areas of your life you need to work on. Life is, of course, a jigsaw. How the separate aspects fit together in a person's life is what's important, but the constituent parts can be developed and improved individually.

	I feel good about this	Neutral	I do not feel good about this
FIVE KEY DRIVERS			
Feeling a general sense of control	☐	☐	☐
Being generally optimistic	☐	☐	☐
Feeling comfortable about the way you look	☐	☐	☐
Believing that people think well of you	☐	☐	☐
Feeling confident about managing in old age	☐	☐	☐
TEN FURTHER DRIVERS			
Satisfaction with partner and sex life	☐	☐	☐
Feeling in good health and having energy	☐	☐	☐
Religious/spiritual beliefs guiding the way you live	☐	☐	☐
Not feeling bored most of the time	☐	☐	☐
A positive working environment	☐	☐	☐
Satisfaction with household finances	☐	☐	☐
A positive childhood	☐	☐	☐
Satisfaction with family relationships and friendship networks	☐	☐	☐
Not feeling life is too stressful	☐	☐	☐
Setting personal goals and working toward them	☐	☐	☐

STRESS-FREE LIVING POINTS 22–25

❍ If you feel down, don't fight it; remember that feeling bad is fine – even necessary – in many circumstances. Just make best use of those feelings to move forward.

❍ To boost your self-esteem in five minutes, list every negative thought you experience about yourself; now cross them out, and replace them with positive phrases. Keep this list.

❍ To cope well with change, start by writing down your hopes and fears. On the same page, list your personal assets. Now realize how your assets will help the situation.

❍ To clear your mind, write down your practical goals; create a time-line with necessary tasks, update it weekly, and watch your achievements grow.

FIVE EXERCISES FOR SELF-KNOWLEDGE

You can feel totally different about yourself if you take some simple actions. Use a notebook to work through these exercises.

1 Communicating positively with ourselves is critical for laying the foundations of a clear and calm life in which we are in control and not just responding to events around us and the needs of others. Having the self-confidence to believe in yourself comes from speaking kindly to yourself, not beating yourself up, not feeling responsible for everything that goes wrong, taking responsibility when it is appropriate, and refusing to allow others to talk down to you. For the next week or two, keep a notebook and write down all the disempowering statements that you make to yourself, or that others say to you, and the circumstances in which these occurred. When you have some quiet time, write down calmer, more appropriate, responses that help rather than hinder you.

2 Cut through all the clutter to see the way forward. Identify one or two aims (preferably not overlarge aims, but small to medium-size ones). Write these down. Now write down small steps along the way to realizing your aims. Make a time-line by working out when each step can reasonably be achieved, and then audit this time-line regularly. You can now simplify your goals and aims into manageable and achievable challenges and begin to feel good about making progress.

3 It is unrealistic to expect life to be one long road of joy and calmness. You have to ask yourself why negative emotions exist at all. Why do we experience anger, jealousy, fear, embarrassment, loneliness, or depression? Instead of suppressing such emotions, we sometimes need to allow ourselves to feel them, because we learn from this process – it helps us establish what we will or will not accept in the future. Benefiting from negative emotions is all a question of balance. To feel low for a while in the face of adversity is a process. To be clinically depressed, or overanxious, is also a process, but a much more drastic one. Understanding the difference between these and stopping the more serious one from taking over your life is what is important. Allowing yourself to feel negative feelings is fine in the right circumstances. They might even be a driving force to take you forward. Think back over your past and identify times when you have felt sad, gloomy, or lethargic. Think about what happened when you overcame these feelings. Now write these thoughts down. The next time that you are feeling bad, look at your notes and remember that there were times in your life when you felt similar feelings and yet you won through.

4 If you want to make changes in your life, what has stopped you in the past? Is it something that might stop you in the future? Note down the answers to these questions that occur to you. Ask yourself next what your assets in life are, and write down your answers. Think of how your assets can help you overcome problems. This exercise helps you tackle future obstacles more effectively.

5 If you want to overcome a problem, it can help to depersonalize it. Imagine what you would say if you were going to offer advice to a friend – this might be much easier. Write down each statement you make, giving a response to each. Make sure that they are objective and unclouded by your own emotions, which are probably affecting your judgment.

your
BODY

10 steps to vitality

For vitality you need energy – an all-too-elusive commodity. When you simplify your health regime, and your life, you free up energy for creative, inspiring pursuits. Everything you need to make positive and simple changes to your health routine is covered in this section. Here are ten ways to bring vitality into your life.

1 BEAT THE BLUES

Physical activity releases endorphins (pleasure chemicals) in the brain. By exercising – even for just 15 minutes at a time – you can change the way you feel. If you tend to lack resolve, just substitute one activity for another: walk briskly instead of driving to the store, or go out dancing instead of to the movies.

2 SNACK ATTACK

When you feel the need for an energy boost, give your body nutrients to work with. Eating well is the surest way to increase vitality. Well-chosen snacks can be just as enticing as junk food, and wholesome as well. Stock up on dried fruit and fresh nuts; wholewheat breadsticks with dips; yogurt and fresh fruit; smoothies and fresh juices.

3 QUELL SUGAR CRAVINGS

Sugar gives us energy – we all know that. Well, yes and no. Sugar gives a fast-acting energy boost which is why it is so seductive and popular in snacks. But when the sugar is used up, we are primed to crave more. Slow-releasing carbohydrates give a better balance of steady energy that is usable over a sustained period of time. Satisfy a sweet tooth with chocolate that has 70 percent cocoa solids, as this type has less sugar.

4 WAKE-UP CALLS

Incorporate instant wake-up tricks for when you feel yourself slowing down. Splash cold water on your face; or lie down with a cooling gel-filled eye mask on your eyes to freshen up. For a kind of head massage, run your fingers and palms through your hair and take a firm hold of large sections on either side of your head. Grasp

> When life gives you oranges, enjoy. When life gives you lemons, make lemonade.

the sections firmly and tug gently, pulling your scalp. Release and repeat over the rest of your head for a couple of minutes.

5 VITALITY IN A GLASS

The easiest way to capture vitality is to drink juices packed with the life force of plants. Raw fruits and vegetables are loaded with energy-giving nutrients and enzymes. Make yourself a large glass of fresh juice every day. Try any of the following: a green apple and watermelon crush (include the seeds and some washed skin); a mango, carrot, and ginger "zinger"; or a raspberry, orange, and banana smoothie (made with crushed ice).

6 FUN TIME

Life isn't all serious. When you laugh from the heart and are enjoying yourself, you have much more energy. Look for what is good about a situation. Also, every so often do something you enjoy, even if only for 10 minutes. You'll feel a lot livelier.

7 SLEEP CURE

You know how much sleep you need – now you just need to make sure you get it.

Too little sleep drags you down, while too much has a soporific effect. Train yourself by observing regular hours. Avoid caffeine, arguments, and high-energy television shows late at night. Alcohol stops you from getting to a deep level of sleep, and dehydration can lead to midnight waking, so sip water all day.

8 CUT THE CAFFEINE

Caffeine can pep you up in the short term, but in the long term it leads to a fuzzy brain and low energy, until the next "fix." It is the most widely consumed drug in the world. Replace coffee with coffee substitutes made from chicory, barley, or dandelion. Drink weak or decaffeinated tea, green tea, herbal or fruit teas, or hot water with lemon and honey.

9 PLAN FOR THE GOOD THINGS

Do an audit of what is good about the day and what you can look forward to tomorrow. If nothing springs to mind, that is a message that you need to plan something nice. This helps you feel forward-looking and optimistic.

10 VITAMIN VITALITY

Take a good-quality vitamin and mineral supplement daily as insurance against any deficiencies or to make up for any dietary transgressions.

energy exercise

We are designed to be active – it makes us feel good both physically and mentally. Our modern, sedentary lifestyle does us no favors; however, despite today's laborsaving lifestyle, you can greatly improve your activity level by making small adjustments to your daily routine and finding time for invigorating exercise.

If you are truly time-poor, incorporate the 5–10 minute exercise routines (see Stress-Free Living Points 26–32, opposite) at any time of day. Work through just one, or a combination: each will refresh and invigorate you. Just at the moment when you feel like slumping into a chair, take a few minutes for a pick-me-up workout and you will be raring to go for the next couple of hours.

But you may feel you need to do a bit more. First decide whether you need more exercise, next convince yourself of the benefits (belief is everything), and then get moving. If you've never managed to get past "Go" or to keep yourself motivated for more than a couple of months, work through these tips.

DO YOU GET ENOUGH EXERCISE?

● Can you walk rapidly up three flights of stairs without getting out of breath?
● Do you spend half an hour during the course of your day being active – say, walking briskly or cycling?
● Is your job physically demanding?
● Do you have an acceptable weight/height ratio? Check with your doctor.

If you have ticked three or four, you are doing fine. If you ticked two, you could improve the situation, and if you ticked zero to one, you definitely need to start exercising now. Always consult your medical adviser to assess the suitability of your exercise plan.

FIVE REASONS TO START TODAY

● Cardiovascular health – The more you exercise, the stronger your heart becomes, the more endurance you have, and the smaller your risk of cardiovascular disease.

● Weight management – No weight-control program is complete without a commitment to exercise. If you are doing regular exercise and your body is toning up, yet you do not seem to be losing weight on the scales, remain positive – muscle weighs more than fat.

● Joint flexibility – Use it or lose it. Keep moving all your joints through their full range of motion on a regular basis to help avoid pulled muscles, back problems, and age-related stiffness.

● Reduced cancer risk – Most cancers are related to lifestyle factors and some, particularly breast cancer, have a close link to lack of exercise.

● Mental health – It is well established that mental health problems such as depression and anxiety respond well to a routine of regular physical activity.

THREE GOALS

There are three main physical goals of exercise, and we need to work on part of each on a regular basis. Even athletes who compete mainly in just one field will make sure that they build the other elements into their programs as well.

● Suppleness/grace – Watch retired dancers in their later years and notice what a bonus good posture and supple-ness are. Good for suppleness: yoga, ballet, t'ai chi, gymnastics.

● Stamina/endurance – You are working to your peak and building up stamina if you are feeling a little breathless and are working up a light sweat while you exercise, but are still able to hold a conversation. Good for stamina: long-distance brisk walking, cycling, running, swimming, team games, racket games, jumping rope, dancing.

● Strength – Some people are put off strength training, but you don't have to be a professional athlete to be strong. Good for strength: weight training, cycling, rowing.

STRESS-FREE LIVING POINTS 26–32

❍ Buy a jump rope and start using it. Jumping rope is quite a vigorous workout and you may only manage a minute or two initially, but you can build it up gradually to five minutes.

❍ Do a 5–10 minute stretch routine or yoga stretches (see pages 14–17).

❍ Cycle for 10 minutes en route to the grocery store and back, once a day.

❍ Invest in a rebounder (a small trampoline) and bounce up and down on it in front of the television for 5–10 minutes.

❍ Practice stomach crunches for 5 minutes. Do them properly to protect your back – you should be working only your stomach muscles in isolation and not your back or neck muscles. Lie flat on your back, feet flat on the floor with knees bent. Cradle your head with your hands behind your neck. Pull in your abdominal muscles and lift your head off the floor. Now take your head farther up toward your knees in short bursts without collapsing on the floor. Don't tuck in your chin – you need to keep a gap between it and your neck. Repeat this 20 times. Now take your left elbow toward your right knee 20 times and then your right elbow toward your left knee 20 times.

❍ Take a one-day introductory course to t'ai chi. Stand in an open space and do your 10-minute routine.

❍ Most people can fit walking into their day, and raising the tempo turns it into a workout. A 20-minute brisk walk to and from your workplace is great exercise for the heart and lungs.

MENTAL GYMNASTICS

By imagining specific muscles being exercised, you can actually strengthen large muscle groups. This sounds like a couch potato's dream, but recent studies have suggested that there is some truth in it (though it may be best not to rely completely on this method). In the studies, the volunteers, in their 20s and 30s, imagined flexing their biceps as hard as possible in specific training sessions five times a week. They were monitored to make sure they were not actually flexing these muscles. They averaged a 13.5 percent increase in strength after just a few weeks – and the gain was maintained three months later. Apparently, neural feedback was making the difference – a remarkable win for the powers of visualization.

Therapists have used visualization for a long time to aid healing and benefit mental health. It is a powerful tool for improving health and wellbeing. With research results such as just cited, sports therapists and trainers are now regularly using the technique to improve athletes' performance. Just by imagining a perfect serve, tennis players are able to improve their performance. By imagining themselves going the extra distance or a bit faster, runners are also benefiting.

To convince yourself of how visualization can work for you, try this quick and easy test to see if you notice any physical benefit. Simply touch your toes, or as near as you can get to your toes (assuming you don't have a bad back), and then straighten up. Now close your eyes and spend a minute visualizing yourself doing this more easily and going farther. You really have to get inside the image and feel and see yourself doing this as accurately as you can. Now touch your toes again and see how well you achieve your goal the second time around.

STRESS-FREE LIVING POINTS 33–37

○ Burn more calories as you exercise. At the pool, wear a foam buoyancy belt that allows you to stay afloat as you jog in the water – the water resistance helps you burn over 11 calories per minute, with no damage to joints.

○ Practice the workplace workout. Keep a Dynaband at the office and spend a few minutes curling your arms or, if you can stretch out on the floor, doing leg scissors against the resistance.

○ Stay motivated – and enjoy team spirit. By joining a group of like-minded people you will be more enthused about getting out of bed on Sunday morning for a game – and it could do wonders for your social life as well as your fitness levels. Look into softball, soccer, volleyball, hockey, basketball, or any team sport.

○ Increase the benefits of day-to-day activities. For instance, when you are on the phone, stretch your arm or leg muscles, or do some buttock crunches. Keep a tennis ball by the phone, so you can place it between your knees and squeeze your legs together to work the inner thigh muscles while you chat.

○ Adapt your fitness routine. Sometimes changes in the seasons or circumstances cause good intentions to fizzle out. If your life changes – perhaps you work a different shift, or your workload increases for a while – you will need to find new ways of accommodating your fitness plan. More subtle, however, is the effect that the seasons have on our energy levels and desire to work out. A hot gym is not very enticing in high summer, and jogging on a cold, rainy morning probably does not appeal either. Learn to adapt your routine and you will keep it beneficial.

the water cure

Water has been used therapeutically since time immemorial. The savannahs of today were actually the coastlines of long ago and many researchers believe that we evolved from semiaquatic forebears. Literally the liquid of life, water can be used both internally and externally to heal, revive, and replenish us.

STRESS-FREE LIVING POINTS 38–43

❍ Healing ways with water include starting the day with a glass of lukewarm water and a squeeze of lemon to help flush the liver out and aid digestion.

❍ Increase your daily water intake by carrying around a pint (500ml) bottle filled with fresh water; drink and refill it four times a day to meet your target.

❍ A final rinse of cold water after a shower will tighten facial pores, improve skin tone on the body, and help to improve circulation.

❍ Chopped fresh herbs such as lavender poured into a running bath make a delightful aromatherapy soak for relaxation; or try chopped fresh fruit such as oranges and lemons in a cool bath for an exfoliating burst of zest and energy.

❍ When out on the town, alternate an alcoholic drink with a glass of spring water to reduce the chances of a morning hangover.

❍ Always keep water at your desk and by your bed, to sip whenever you are thirsty.

We are composed of over 70 percent water, which means it is essential for our very lives. After air, water is our single most important nutrient, without which we cannot survive for more than a few days. Whether liquid, ice, or steam, all the alternative states of water have strong therapeutic benefits. A steam bath at a spa is luxury in itself, but you can enjoy similar benefits at home by filling a basin with steaming hot water and inhaling scents such as eucalyptus, mint, or thyme. A cold compress applied to a hot brow can be tremendously soothing. Because water is literally "on tap," we tend to undervalue its importance, which is why it's worth taking a new look at this life-giver.

YOU MAY NEED TO DRINK MORE WATER:

- If your urine is darker than a light straw or lemon color
- In the summer when you perspire more
- Before, during, and after exercise
- If your office is air-conditioned or centrally-heated
- If you are breast-feeding, to replace lost liquid
- When you are constipated
- If you have loose bowels, to replace lost water
- If you have a dry-skin condition
- If you regularly experience headaches
- If you have aching joints
- If you have benign prostate problems
- If you are prone to kidney stones

DRINK UP

For perfect skin and maximum vitality, all models, sports people, and performers know that they must drink two quarts (liters) of water daily. Anybody with even the mildest nagging complaint – headaches, dry skin, digestive problems, bad breath, poor wound healing – will probably benefit from drinking more. Stick to plain water, jazzed up if necessary with a little juice or an infusion, but do not count coffee, strong tea, colas, or alcohol in your daily allowance. Keep a pint (500ml) bottle with you at all times and empty it four times a day. The difference after a couple of weeks will be noticeable.

RELAX

You can dissolve various minerals and herbs in your bath-water to help yourself relax. Add a large handful of sea salt or Epsom salts to your bath (or to a foot bath). This will help to draw out impurities from your skin. A large handful of oats or lavender added to bathwater will help soothe itchy skin conditions or, in summer, mild sunburn.

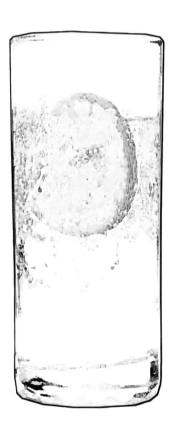

how to detox

A detox is a time when you alter your food and drink intake and ideally take a bit more rest. The aim is to give your body a breathing space by easing the load on your metabolism and give your liver and other detoxification organs less work to do.

The traditional time to do a detox is in spring or early fall. As the seasons change, so do your body's needs. A three-day detox helps clean out your system and prepare your body for the coming months. If you feel good about doing these clear-outs, you could also do another three-day detox as a booster halfway through the season, say just prior to the winter holidays, or before your summer vacation.

The body has a natural ability to detoxify substances that are harmful to it, if they are allowed to build up. These include by-products of everyday foods. In the normal course of events, and assuming that diet and exercise are reasonably healthy, special measures are not needed. However, we live in an age that encourages toxins to build up and threaten the body.

Sources include:

TOXINS WE CONSUME – from food processing and additives as well as from too much coffee or alcohol.
TOXINS PRODUCED IN THE BODY – by-products of metabolism and disturbed digestive health.
HEAVY METALS – such as lead and cadmium from gasoline, cigarette smoke, and other sources.
POLLUTION – from a wide variety of sources including the 60,000 chemicals in common use in farming and industry.

The principles of fasting and detoxing have been used since time immemorial as a healing tool. The practice of fasting – eating sparingly or avoiding certain foods at particular times – is even enshrined within most major religions, for example at Lent, Passover, and Ramadan. While a short detox cannot claim to eliminate all accumulated toxins, it can help to redress the balance, give a sense of wellbeing, put you back in control of your health, and spur you on to make longer-lasting, positive changes.

FOODS TO INCLUDE ON A DETOX

● The main foods to increase on a detox are vegetables and fruits. As they are fibrous and watery, they are the main building blocks of a detox program. Follow any of the serving suggestions below, and include fruit and vegetables in every meal.

● Drink mainly fruit and herbal teas. Some teas in particular can help to improve the effects of a detox. Experiment with dandelion, nettle, vervain, slippery elm, chamomile, marshmallow, fennel, and meadowsweet.

● Instead of wheat, use products made from other grains such as oats, rye, barley, rice, corn, buckwheat, millet, and quinoa. Some people feel better if they also restrict oats, rye, corn, and barley and stick to the other grains. A wide variety of common breakfast cereals, crackers, rice cakes, pastas, and baked goods include these grains.

● Soya or rice milk is to be used instead of cow's milk. Choose calcium-enriched versions if you wish. A wide variety of dishes can be cooked with either, and soya yogurts, desserts, and cheeses are available. If soya milk does not agree with you (it doesn't with some people), stick to rice milk.

● For sweetening, use a little honey if you wish. It's best to choose naturally sweet fruits and their purées.

● If you are eating meats then stick to white fish, oily fish, lean chicken, or game.

● Plant proteins are great to use instead of animal proteins. These include lentils, beans, soya foods, nuts, and seeds.

FOODS TO EXCLUDE ON A DETOX

● Coffee and tea – even decaffeinated.

● All colas and flavored sodas.

● All alcohol.

● Refined sugar and sugary foods.

● All wheat-based foods and products, including breads, crackers, cereals, pasta, pastries, cakes, cookies, and batter (check the labels of all these to see if wheat is included or not).

● All cow's milk products, including milk, cheeses, butter, and cream. Because cow's milk yogurt is predigested to a large degree by the live bacteria it contains, plain yogurt can often be included in a detox. You could also have a little goat's or sheep's milk cheese once a day.

● Some people prefer to avoid all meat on a detox as it can be a little hard to digest.

● Very fatty foods (apart from avocados, nuts, and seeds in limited quantities) and all processed or fast foods.

WARM-SEASON DETOX PLAN

A detox lends itself naturally to the warm months, when an abundant choice of fruits and vegetables tempts us, and when it is easier to eat light meals. Aim to make at least 50 percent of your meals from raw ingredients such as fresh vegetables and fruits.

Summer serving suggestions

● Start the day with hot water and lemon, the classic detox drink (it helps to promote liver function).

● Breakfast can start with two portions of fruit sliced attractively on a plate, followed by something more filling.

● Summer is salad season, so get adventurous with grating, chopping, and slicing. For variety, add roasted vegetables.

● Cold soups are another great way to get raw vegetables into your diet. Gazpacho (usually made from raw tomatoes and bell peppers) is the classic summer soup, but cucumber and mint soup is also delicious.

● Summertime and the juicing is easy. Invest in a juicer and get carried away. Carrot and apple are good bases to which you can add almost any other fruit or vegetable depending on your mood. Sip the juice slowly when detoxing to avoid a sugar rush.

● Simple meals of fish or chicken, sprinkled with lemon and enjoyed with lightly steamed vegetables and a side salad, are ideal summer detox fare at a restaurant.

● Summer berries made into exotic salads, fools, or compotes are delicious – enjoy them while the sun shines. Try broiled (grilled) fresh fruit slices too.

COLD-SEASON DETOX PLAN

As the days shorten and we wrap up in more layers, warm foods become more appealing. Adapting your detox plan to this season means eating more filling and warming foods.

Winter serving suggestions

● Start each day with a warm drink. Choose hot blackcurrant or cranberry to give you a winter boost of vitamin C.

● Breakfasts could include warm cereals. As an alternative to the more familiar hot oatmeal (porridge), have a bowl of breakfast rice (cooked brown rice) or millet porridge. Make these with soya or rice milk as an alternative to cow's milk. Add all sorts of toppings: mashed banana, diced dried fruit, raisins, chopped unsalted nuts, grated coconut, or blueberries (frozen and defrosted).

● Soups are comforting and filling, and vegetable-based soups are an ideal way to make sure you get your winter quota of antioxidants.

● A warm winter-vegetable stir-fry served with brown rice is an ideal cold-weather alternative to a salad.

● Make warm bean dips by mashing up cooked beans such as pinto beans, adding chopped herbs, and dressing them with lemon and olive oil. Serve the dips with wheat-free crackers.

● Prepare buckwheat noodles with black olives, red peppers, sun-dried tomatoes, basil, and goat's milk cheese.

● Baked apples cooked in fruit juice and stuffed with dried apricots are an ideal winter treat, topped with soya yogurt.

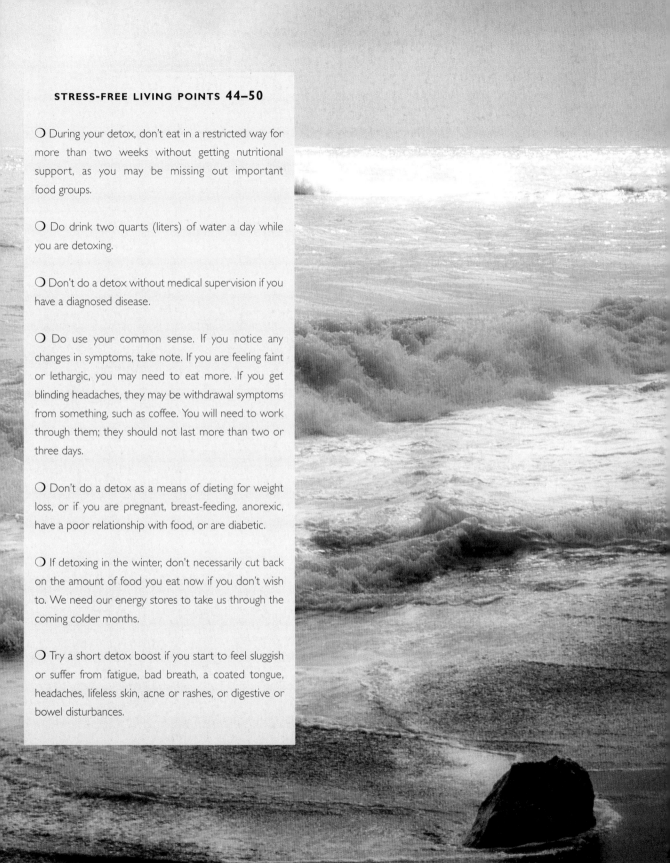

STRESS-FREE LIVING POINTS 44–50

❍ During your detox, don't eat in a restricted way for more than two weeks without getting nutritional support, as you may be missing out important food groups.

❍ Do drink two quarts (liters) of water a day while you are detoxing.

❍ Don't do a detox without medical supervision if you have a diagnosed disease.

❍ Do use your common sense. If you notice any changes in symptoms, take note. If you are feeling faint or lethargic, you may need to eat more. If you get blinding headaches, they may be withdrawal symptoms from something, such as coffee. You will need to work through them; they should not last more than two or three days.

❍ Don't do a detox as a means of dieting for weight loss, or if you are pregnant, breast-feeding, anorexic, have a poor relationship with food, or are diabetic.

❍ If detoxing in the winter, don't necessarily cut back on the amount of food you eat now if you don't wish to. We need our energy stores to take us through the coming colder months.

❍ Try a short detox boost if you start to feel sluggish or suffer from fatigue, bad breath, a coated tongue, headaches, lifeless skin, acne or rashes, or digestive or bowel disturbances.

your
home spa

Going to a spa is a wonderful treat from time to time. But if time or budgetary constraints do not allow for this luxury, you can easily incorporate spa principles into your home routine. Think of pampering yourself as a big treat that you richly deserve, rather than as another chore to add to the list. Use your home spa as a retreat from the bustle of life.

If your bathroom and bedroom, the key players in your spa routine, are uninspiring, now is the time to organize them.

● Use cool neutral colors – paint the bathroom white or cream and splurge on lots of soft, stone-colored, extra-large bath towels.

● Throw away all your old tubes and pots that you have not used for ages; they clutter up the bathroom, and are also probably past their best.

● Buy several stacking basketweave boxes to store all your necessary items – one for creams, one for manicure equipment, one for hair styling, and so on.

● Make sure your bathroom and bedroom are clean and fresh – open the window a few inches if you can.

● Make a shopping list of the items that will make your home spa trouble-free – mud face masks, sea salt for your bath, rich creams for your feet, wax strips, and so on.

Devise a rotating program of nice things you like to do for yourself. Perhaps you might need a professional visit or two to get you started – it is easier to keep your eyebrows shaped once they have been done by a professional, and it's easier to keep your feet trouble-free after a visit to a pedicurist.

Don't be overambitious – if you cram in too much in search of the new-look you, you will become overwhelmed – better to do a few things well. One possibility is to set aside pampering time twice a week, and tackle all your health and beauty jobs in one go. Or you could indulge in a whole day when you take the phone off the hook, stock up with witch hazel and cotton balls for soothing eye pads, and enjoy a total immersion in luxury. You could also combine a day like this with a detox (see pages 38–41).

Here are some delicious ideas for your home spa:

YOGURT CLEANSER – Use plain, live yogurt as a simple cleanser, rubbing it on and splashing it off with water. Not only is it mild and gentle, but it also helps keep skin acidity at the right level.

FUN FACIAL – Mix ½ cup (200g) manuka honey with 10 drops of fresh lime or lemon juice. Wet your face with a warm washcloth, then massage the mask into your skin. Lie back and place thin slices of peeled cucumber, overlapping, all over the mask. Relax for 15 minutes. Wash off the mask, pat your face dry, and apply moisturizer. Honey hydrates the skin and manuka honey has antibacterial properties that help heal skin conditions.

NATURAL SKIN NOURISHER – Both almond oil and avocado oil are ideal skin nourishers. Apply a small amount of one to your skin, and leave it to sink in overnight. Don't forget other areas of skin such as your legs and arms.

DRY-SKIN TREATMENT – For very dry skin conditions, such as eczema, use evening primrose or borage oil. As well as taking this internally you can also pierce a capsule and rub the oil into the affected area for more direct delivery.

FEET FIRST – In the absence of asses' milk (à la Cleopatra) warm up ½ cup (200ml) of whole milk. Add a few mint leaves and a few rosemary leaves and stems, and simmer for 15 minutes. Allow to cool. Soak two large washcloths in the mixture and wrap one around each foot for 15 minutes while relaxing. (Put a clean towel under your feet to avoid making a mess.)

HAIR HELP – Start with 2 tablespoons of apricot kernel, wheatgerm, olive, or grapeseed oil, and add the following essential oils: 4 drops of chamomile, 4 drops of ylang-ylang, 2 drops of sandalwood, and 5 drops of rose. Apply the mixture to your hair and give yourself a deep scalp massage. Rub more of the oil mixture into the ends of your hair. Wrap your head in a warm damp towel and lie down for 15 minutes. (Make maximum use of the session by wearing a face mask at the same time.) Shampoo and condition your hair as normal (you may need two shampoos to get all the oil out).

energy foods

One of the most common complaints is to be lacking energy. Although energy is definable, it is not easy to describe. At a nutritional level we get the energy we need from carbohydrates and from stored fats in our bodies. We also need certain nutrients, such as B vitamins, vitamin C, and magnesium, to turn carbohydrates and fats into usable energy. However, energy is also mental energy, enthusiasm for life, and our very life force. Unfortunately, these can't be bottled, but certainly if you are feeling physically vital, because you are eating in tune with your body and with the seasons – in other words, in tune with nature – then you can more easily capture these other, magical energies.

VITAMINS AND MINERALS

Grains, fortified cereals, leafy green vegetables, eggs, liver, and brewer's yeast are all sources of B VITAMINS. This family of vitamins is needed for all steps of the energy-production cycle.

We get VITAMIN C from fruits and vegetables. The citric-acid cycle, so named because it is dependent on vitamin C, is a fundamental part of the energy-production cycle in all cells. Most animals make large amounts of this vitamin but humans have lost the ability to do so, probably because our ancestors thrived on diets high in sources of vitamin C.

All green leafy vegetables are also sources of the energy mineral MAGNESIUM. Include one portion daily. Other magnesium-rich foods include nuts, seeds, eggplant (aubergine), and popcorn.

CARBOHYDRATES

Complex carbohydrates that release slow-burning fuel are better than carbohydrates that release fuel rapidly – for a quick fix followed by a quick burnout. To make the wisest choices see the chart below.

We all have different metabolisms. Some people seem to thrive on diets that are loaded with healthy complex carbohydrates such as brown rice and oats. Others, however, need to reduce these sources of carbohydrates in their diet, because grains do not agree with them and sap their energy. For these people in particular, legumes, vegetables, and fruits remain valuable sources of carbohydrates and therefore need to be increased in the diet accordingly.

REDUCE THESE SOURCES OF CARBOHYDRATES

- Cordials, squashes, colas
- White bread, products containing white flour, crackers
- White rice
- Sugary breakfast cereals
- Candy, sugary yogurts, sugary desserts

INCREASE THESE SOURCES OF CARBOHYDRATES

- Fresh fruit and vegetables, fresh fruit juices (appropriately diluted), fresh vegetable juices
- Wholewheat bread, oatcakes, rye crackers
- Brown rice, quinoa, barley, kasha, buckwheat
- Rolled oats, wholegrain air-popped cereals, granola, oat flapjacks (homemade)
- Chocolate with 70 percent cocoa solids

SUNSHINE FOODS

● In the summer there is such a variety of fruits and vege-tables that you can enjoy summer juices daily. They make great pick-me-ups mid-afternoon instead of coffee or tea.

● Chilled soups like gazpacho, cucumber, and watercress soups are refreshing in hot weather.

● Enjoy different salads, such as tabbouleh (bulgur mixed with chopped tomatoes, cucumber, onions, parsley, and mint); Waldorf salad (chopped celery, apple, walnut); grilled eggplant (aubergine) with tomato, green onion, cilantro (coriander) leaves, and balsamic vinegar.

● Platters of brightly colored fresh fruit are always a treat for dessert no matter how grand the occasion – for a change, dip the fruits in melted chocolate or in plain yogurt mixed with honey.

WINTER WARMERS

When cold winds are blowing, a large salad may not be the most appealing way for you to eat energy foods. The following serving suggestions will make eating high-energy foods really enjoyable:

● Winter vegetables roasted until they have caramelized to a delicious sweetness are a great way of enjoying these vitality foods. Roast some carrots, parsnips, sweet potato, yam, rutabaga (swede), or celery root (celeriac) with olive oil, lots of garlic, and herbs. Or enjoy roast Mediterranean vegetables like eggplant (aubergine), bell peppers, sun-dried tomatoes, zucchini (courgettes), and olives.

● Warming vegetable soups are high in antioxidants. Try carrot and cilantro (coriander); roast bell pepper and roast tomato; and borscht, a soup made from beets (beetroot).

● Hot oatmeal (porridge) is the ultimate winter breakfast and is loaded with slow-releasing carbohydrates to sustain your energy through the morning. Jazz it up with blue-berries and yogurt, cranberry sauce, or banana and raisins.

● Warm fruit compote, made with soaked dried fruit and spices, is an ideal winter treat.

If you are frequently low in energy, it is important to eliminate or deal with some other possible causes, which could include any of the following:

● Lack of sleep

● Anemia (lack of iron)

● Other nutritional deficiencies

● Low thyroid function

● Depression

● Stress/worry/too much to do

foods that heal

Your body is a remarkable organic machine. It is constantly renewing itself, cell by cell, atom by atom, without you being conscious of it. The only time you become aware of this process is when an added stress is put on this resource, say when you cut or injure yourself or when you are unwell.

It has been firmly established by research that people who are well nourished heal much better than those who are undernourished. Alarmingly, even those who believe themselves to be well nourished, because they get enough calories in their diet, may be lacking in some essential nutrients needed for optimal healing. By giving your body the best-quality raw materials it needs for this ceaseless job, your body will deal more readily with a crisis, and you will be best prepared to cope with ailments as they arise. Regularly including the following foods in your diet can make all the difference:

FRUITS are rich in vitamin C, which is vital for making collagen. This makes up the matrix of our skin and tissues and has to be repaired in case of injury. Extreme vitamin C deficiency shows as the bleeding gums of scurvy, but more subtle deficiencies also impair healing. Fruits rich in vitamin C are citrus, kiwi, strawberries, blackcurrants, guava, and litchis (lychees). Make yourself a berry fruit salad or a fresh juice, chop some fruit and serve it with yogurt, or combine a coulis (see page 95) with homemade fresh fruit ice cream.

OILY FISH and some cold-pressed oils are rich sources of essential fats. Your cell membranes get their flexibility from these essential fats, and making sure you get more of these – rather than saturated fats from meat, cheese, and butter, or hydrogenated fats from margarine or processed foods – results in improved healing. This is particularly true for people with eczema or asthma. Eat two or three portions a week of oily fish: stir-fry fresh tuna strips with garlic and green onions; make mackerel paté by blending cooked mackerel with cottage cheese and lemon; have sardines on toast; enjoy pickled herring fillets (rollmops) with salad. Dress your salads with delicious, nutty oils such as walnut or flax oil.

NUTS AND SEEDS are other sources of essential fats, but they are also excellent sources of zinc and selenium. Zinc is needed for all healing processes, and zinc deficiency can certainly prolong wound-healing and recovery from colds. Selenium helps maintain health by enabling a key antioxidant enzyme to fight toxins. Serve chopped nuts on your morning granola or muesli; sprinkle them on yogurt; enjoy unsalted nuts as a snack with dried fruit; add them to cakes and flapjacks; include sunflower seeds in tossed salads; and stuff vegetables such as peppers or tomatoes with nutty rice.

LEGUMES are also rich in zinc and provide iron, which is needed for building blood. They make an excellent substitute for meat-based dishes once or twice a week. Because they are also so rich in fiber, they are ideal for encouraging healthy digestion and they help lower cholesterol levels. Enjoy lentil soup, bean salad, chilli con carne, casseroles with beans, black-eyed peas and rice, falafel, and other bean-based dishes.

"VITAMIN S" – sleep – though not a food, is vital for healing. Many of the body's repair processes take place at night when you are asleep. If you are deprived of sufficient rest, your body will find it more difficult to heal. Sleep will nourish your body as much as any vital food, so make sure you get your nightly portion.

tune in to your body

You can get the best out of your day without doing anything radically different from normal. By understanding how your body responds at different times of the day you can capitalize on your natural 24-hour cycle, or circadian rhythm, and make the day work for you.

YOUR 24-HOUR BODY CLOCK

To study the body clock, or circadian rhythms, volunteers were put in isolation units without clues as to the time and were fed identical hourly meals. It was found that their bodies still followed clear patterns. These daily rhythms are governed by an internal body clock, which is controlled by various hormones. Temperature, heart rate, metabolic rate, and urinary flow follow distinct patterns throughout a 24-hour period. Knowing this means that you can capitalize on when you feel best by planning your activities around your natural body rhythms. For instance, if you are planning a night out, which will obviously interfere with your body clock, see if you can work a lunchtime nap into your day. Then when you are out on the town, everyone will wonder where you got that extra energy from!

Early morning At about 6 a.m. your body temperature rises. Levels of endorphins (pleasure and pain-killing chemicals in the brain) and cortisol (a hormone produced by the adrenal glands) rise to prepare us for the day ahead. Sex hormones – estrogen and testosterone – are at their peak in the early morning.

Mid-morning We are at our most alert, particularly for cognitive work.

Mid-day Energy levels plummet, and body temperature and adrenaline levels slump for a while. This suggests that a siesta after lunch is something from which everyone could benefit.

Mid-afternoon Body temperature and adrenaline levels rise once more. Cortisol levels even out and then drop. The result is that we are cruising both mentally and physically, while being at our most relaxed.

Early evening Body temperature and adrenaline levels are at their peak. Muscles and joints are most supple, coordination and stamina are at their best, and circulation is working optimally. This means that we benefit most from physical activity at this time.

Mid-evening Levels of melatonin (a hormone secreted by the pineal gland, which is stimulated by darkness and suppressed by light) are beginning to rise, readying us for sleep. Levels of endorphins and anti-inflammatory hormones begin to fall, which means our immunity is at its lowest level.

Late evening We are in a state of mini-hibernation. Our need to drink, eat, and have bathroom breaks is diminished, and our systems tick over until the morning.

Midnight Levels of growth hormones increase to encourage growth processes while we sleep. These occur in very deep, non-dreaming sleep, which alternate through the night with dreaming sleep. Each full cycle lasts about 1½ hours. The restorative (deep) sleep predominates at first (and itself consists of several different levels), while the dreaming stages gradually lengthen as the night progresses, so that dreaming amounts to about two hours a night in total.

Late night At around 3–5 a.m. our body temperature and levels of adrenaline and cortisol are at their lowest, which allow us to sleep deeply and enable body repair mechanisms to work without interruption.

working with your body clock

MAXIMIZE DAYTIME ENERGY

Drink enough liquid through the day and make the most of your body clock for constant energy:

7:30 A.M. A glass of fruit juice helps you to meet one fifth of your daily target for fruit and vegetable intake.

11 A.M. A cup of tea mid-morning can give a mild caffeine boost to aid concentration; it is also rich in antioxidants. The caffeine has plenty of time to work out of your system before nighttime.

12:30 P.M. Replenish your water intake.

3 P.M. To boost blood sugar for the afternoon, enjoy a freshly made vegetable juice such as carrot with ginger.

6 P.M. A glass of your favorite wine helps you to relax after your day.

8 P.M. After dinner, calming mint tea will ease digestion.

11 P.M. To help you sleep, have a drink based on calcium and oats, such as calcium-enriched rice milk warmed up with finely milled oats and a teaspoon of honey.

MORNING

● Leave your curtains open, or have sheer curtains, rather than cutting out light with heavy fabrics. Your body clock works best when it is allowed to react to natural light levels. Light enters the eye and triggers the pineal gland to produce the hormone melatonin, which helps you regulate your waking/sleeping cycle effectively.

● When you get out of bed, do so slowly, rolling onto your elbow and swinging your legs over the bed. Your ligaments are at their most relaxed now (you are an inch taller than when you went to bed) and need to be eased slowly into the day. This is why it is a bad idea to leap across the room in a panic to turn off the alarm.

● Stretch slowly to wake up and while doing so repeat a positive affirmation that you have decided on, such as, "Today, I am strong and able to find solutions when I need them."

● In the shower, finish by alternating short, sharp blasts of very warm water and cold water to get your metabolism working efficiently and to boost circulation, increasing the oxygen flow.

● Eat a nutritious and generous breakfast, or grab something healthy and satisfying on the way to work – do not ever skip breakfast. It's the most important meal of the day.

● Incorporate brisk walking or cycling into your morning commute, for at least one mile (1.5km). You will get into work feeling more positive and refreshed and will already have met half of your exercise commitment for the day.

DAYTIME

- Take the elevator for fewer floors and walk up a couple of flights of stairs. It will become an automatic routine in the end.
- Position a large plant on or very near your desk to mop up indoor toxins. Among the most effective are the dragon tree, ivy, areca palm, Boston fern, weeping fig, peace lily, gerbera, and rubber plant.
- Keep a bottle of water on your desktop and refill it several times a day so that you stay hydrated. Instead of cola or coffee, drink herbal tea or a lemon-and-honey drink.
- Tasks that require logic, short-term memory, or new cognitive skills are best tackled about three hours after you get up in the morning. Jobs that need both mental and physical stamina are best left until the afternoon. If you want to memorize something for the long term, or do your best at a test, do these in the late afternoon.
- At midday go outside and walk around for 15 minutes. Spend another 15 minutes of your lunchtime meditating, to recharge your batteries.
- Make your lunch power-packed with valuable nutrients to sustain you through the afternoon. Avoid coffee, tea, candy, and cookies, which will drain your reserves. Instead, enjoy some of the foods mentioned on pages 44–7.
- Three times a day, have a quiet workout that no one will notice. To help it become a routine, pick specific times, such as coffee breaks. Neck, ankle and wrist rolls, stretches, crunches, and deep breathing are all possible.

EVENING

- Break your routine with a walk home or a workout. This will help you leave behind the worries of the day. Your body's peak time for exercise is between 6 and 7 p.m.
- Take a shower and change your clothes before you do anything else, like cooking supper. Changing the tempo of your day will help you relax.
- Enjoy a glass or two of wine or beer, the antioxidants will do you good and some alcohol can help you to relax early in the evening. Don't drink any more than this, or drink it too late, as it could interfere with your sleep patterns.
- Eat a small evening meal – your metabolism is highest in the morning and lowest in the evening, so eating accordingly will help your body to work at its optimum.
- Spend a few minutes focusing on what has been good about your day and what you have accomplished. Think about just one thing you would like to achieve tomorrow (not more than this or you can start to feel overwhelmed and get anxious). One positive thing each day is 365 positive achievements a year – not bad at all.
- Do some relaxation exercises for 10 minutes late in the evening to prepare yourself for bed. Avoid energetic exercise at this time, as it would make your metabolism race and keep you awake.

your
HOME

50 ways to get organized

Getting organized, and staying that way, is one of the easiest ways to simplify your life. It may seem an insurmountable task initially, but if you tackle one aspect of your organizational needs at a time, making new habits that stick, it will become easy. Really! If you apply these ideas you will find you have more time for the things you enjoy.

TIME MANAGEMENT

1 When taking on new tasks, think through what they will mean to your new sense of organization. Always overestimate rather than underestimate the time involved and if necessary shelve something else – if you try to take on too much at once you will simply get back to your old disorganized self again.

2 Make sure that you use a calendar (with plenty of room to write on each day) or a day-planner. Keep it with you and refer to it often.

3 Deal with things when they crop up. If this is not practical, make a note on your calendar or in your day-planner on the appropriate date and make a point of dealing with it then.

4 Delegate if you can. You can't possibly do everything, so judicious chore-division is often necessary.

5 Open your mail first thing and immediately get rid of anything you don't need, such as envelopes and junk mail. Don't let it pile up.

6 Set yourself a time limit to complete a particular task. If you overshoot, make another time slot to work on it. You will learn to control time rather than allowing it to control you.

7 Keep a stack of jobs to do, along with the equipment needed, such as your sewing box or manicure kit, in a drawer or cupboard near the television.

> Nothing is a waste of time if you use the experience wisely.

KEEP ONE STEP AHEAD

8 Before you leave an area, allow a few extra minutes to clear it up – stack newspapers, clear the kitchen counter, or tidy up your desk. You will feel better when you return to it.

9 To make clearing up easier, make sure you have the right types of shelves, boxes, and storage systems: a newspaper rack, a pot for pens, a CD rack, and so on.

10 Write down phone numbers and addresses immediately in your phone book or personal organizer – you will avoid endless hours fruitlessly searching for them when you need them.

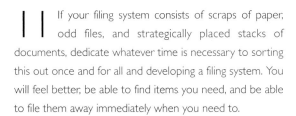

11 If your filing system consists of scraps of paper, odd files, and strategically placed stacks of documents, dedicate whatever time is necessary to sorting this out once and for all and developing a filing system. You will feel better, be able to find items you need, and be able to file them away immediately when you need to.

12 Keep pegboards for keys, bulletin boards for phone messages, and racks for shoes and umbrellas.

13 Make a list of things you regularly use in the house – soap, shampoo, cans of beans, paper towels – and bulk-buy them once a month.

14 Keep a folder for appliance guarantees and instruction manuals so that they are easily to hand.

15 Purge your filing system regularly – the result can be very satisfying.

16 Keep important documents and difficult-to-replace items in a fire-retardant box.

GO WITH THE FLOW

17 Work out when you are most energetic, most creative, most reflective, and also work out when you are most in need of a rest, and plan your activities accordingly to suit these times (see pages 48–51).

18 If changes occur, be flexible and adapt; fighting new situations can just lead to frustration.

19 Work out what your time is worth. It may be more economical to get things delivered or to hire help – if you use the saved time wisely.

20 The effective use of time includes taking it easy to recharge your batteries when needed.

21 If you live in a multi-person household, make a plan for others to help out. If they don't do their share, don't let it bother you – life is too short. Threaten to hire a cleaner and make the others pay for it.

22 Weekends are weekends – not time to catch up. Ignore jobs to do and take a mini-break if you can.

MAKE LIFE EASY

23 Get your finances into shape and then set up direct debits for all your bills. You will avoid paying interest charges on overdue bills and can get discounts this way.

24 Live as close to your work as you are able, or work from home as often as you can. Commuting is a great waste of time, money, and energy and certainly does not simplify your life.

25 Get rid of things you don't need or like – see pages 58–60 for tips on how to declutter your life.

26 Say no if you mean no. If you are uncertain, say that you'll think about it and will get back to the other person by a certain time. Stick to what you've said.

27 Keep a special phone book by your phone with all the numbers of utilities, the doctor's office, babysitters, tradespeople, and repair services so that you can reach them quickly in an emergency.

28 Keep a calendar with birthdays and anniversaries marked on it. Refer to it regularly.

29 Keep stocks of birthday presents, small gifts, wrapping paper, and cards for all occasions.

30 Hang on to financial records for only as long as required for accounts, taxes, or other purposes.

31 Keep two separate laundry baskets – one for white and one for colored items.

32 Purge your wardrobe. Get rid of clothing that doesn't fit; repair or clean items that need it, so that everything is always ready to be worn.

33 Sort your remaining clothes by color or season or type – choose any system that works for you, and then stick to it.

GET THE JOB DONE

34 Avoid brooding about jobs to do. Get into the habit of doing something constructive.

35 If you tend to procrastinate, make yourself write down the pros and cons of a situation and reflect on them until you make a decision.

36 Instead of procrastinating about how huge a job seems, do at least something toward it now – and see how much better you feel.

37 If a job seems insurmountably big, divide it into manageable, bite-size tasks and set an agenda for these individual items.

38 If you are unsure of where to start, ask for help or do some research. People can be very supportive.

39 Get your calendar or day-planner out and write deadlines and milestones in it.

40 Reward yourself each step of the way. Not only is this more enjoyable, but it will also produce a sense of achievement, which will keep you motivated.

ROUTINES WORK

41 Decide realistically when you need to leave work, and then stick to it as far as you reasonably can.

42 Get into a regular bedtime routine to improve your chances of getting enough sleep. The routine will also help combat sleeping problems.

43 Work out a two-weekly menu plan – whenever you are feeling uninspired about what to feed your family or friends, thinking "Thursday is stir-fry day" will make it much easier.

44 If you go out to work, make a two-weekly wardrobe plan – gray suit on Monday, blue skirt and pink shirt on Tuesday, and so on. Two weeks gives you plenty of time to get things cleaned.

45 Go through one drawer/bag/shelf each week, weed out the contents and sort out what is left.

46 Clean one kitchen cabinet, closet, cupboard, or shelf in the garage or shed in turn so that the cleaning doesn't build up.

47 Exercise first thing – your day won't interfere with your good intentions – and you will stay fit.

SEASONAL HARMONY

48 Don't fight the seasons. When it is cold, sort out backlog indoors. When it is sunny, work outside.

49 If you can go on vacation at off-peak times you will avoid fighting the crowds.

50 Make your food budget work better by buying seasonal local produce, which will be cheaper and fresher; buy extra to freeze.

make the most
of what you have

Focus on what you have, not on what you don't have. Make the most
of your assets, on every level, and you will never be without.

Making the most of what you have is a state of mind. The age in which we live dictates that we are constantly enticed to be dissatisfied with our lot, to seek more, bigger, or better in all spheres of life. Don't like your sofa? Buy a new one! Need a break? Go on an expensive vacation! Fed up with your domestic life? Get a divorce! If you can make yourself take a step back from this attitude, you can win on many fronts – including self-esteem, finances, and time.

Making the most of what you have means capitalizing on your assets and appreciating what you do have. What it does not imply is being without ambitions or dreams, putting up with second-best, or staying in unrewarding situations because of fear of stepping out into the unknown.

HOME AND ENVIRONMENT

● Unless you have unlimited funds, there comes a point when you need to make the best of your surroundings. It is worth investing in a few interior decorating books or magazines to see how you can recycle what you have, perhaps with a lick of paint or with some clever rearranging. What initially seems like junk can often very easily be turned into a star item if you develop an eye for what works. Mount painted wooden crates on walls as bookshelves, turn a special vase into a lamp, or use lovely old fabrics for unique window shades. If you are not confident about your ability to mix and match in this way, go for simplicity and remember that "less is more."

● Instead of trawling around the shops and spending more money, spend time ruthlessly purging your wardrobe. Get a friend, whose judgment you trust, to help you sort through your clothes and stop you from hanging on to items for the wrong reasons. Change buttons, take up hemlines, and match items in novel ways (lace with tweed, leather with silk) to create a whole new look.

PHYSICAL AND PERSONALITY ASSETS

● None of us is perfect. Instead of focusing on what you do not like about yourself, concentrate on what you do like – your shoulders, your smile, your amusing wit, your thoughtfulness to others. If you acknowledge your good points and accentuate them, you will be less concerned about other aspects.

● What makes you tick? If you really enjoy something, if you are enthusiastic and knowledgeable about it, and if you want to learn more, use this asset to enhance your home, workplace, and leisure.

RELATIONSHIPS

● Instead of dwelling on the shortcomings of those you live with, work on seeing what is good about them and appreciating them for those assets. Remind yourself of what you liked about them in the first place and what they mean to you emotionally. See them in a more positive light and the chances are that they will respond in kind.

● If you need help, ask for it. Work out how those around you can provide support when you need it – and don't be afraid to ask in times of need.

de-junking

and space clearing

It's time to get ruthless! If you really do want to simplify your life, getting rid of debris and clutter that weigh you down is probably one of the most important things you need to do. One of the main reasons this is so important is that it is virtually impossible to see what is really important if you are surrounded by clutter. This disorganization will only engender feelings of frustration and dissatisfaction.

In one sense, getting rid of the clutter is the simplest of solutions – what could be easier as long as you set aside the time? However, in practice, we can always find more important jobs to do, endless other reasons to procrastinate, and, when we finally get down to it, an excessive attachment to all sorts of things for all sorts of reasons, many of which are irrational.

You may find that the need to de-junk applies to all areas of your home, or just to certain areas where you have a "blind-spot." For instance, your desk may be the picture of efficiency, while your home is a mess – or vice versa. If this is the case, then you know you have the skills to get control and you will only have to reorganize your priorities a little bit.

DE-JUNKING STRATEGIES
● Make a list of all the hot spots where clutter builds up – windowsills, bottom drawers, bedside tables, the attic, the entrance hall, and so on. Have a mammoth clear-up of each of these in turn and then do something innovative to stop the buildup again. Put flowers and plants on the windowsills, allocate the bottom drawer to your stamp collection, get rid of the bedside tables (mount lights on the wall by your bed), put shelves up in the attic, put a statue in the entrance hall – whatever works for you.

● Don't be daunted by how much needs to be done. Tackle one small job at a time and every task completed will be a tangible victory. Keep at it: one hour of de-junking does not a designer-attic make, but many hours might.

● If necessary, enlist help. Sometimes it is hard to be detached enough to recognize what is really necessary and what is an attachment that is overdue to be severed.

● If you absolutely have to hire some help, do so – if you are never really going to get those shelves up, paying someone to do it may be what is needed. It may be worth the expense if you will no longer have the chore to do.

● Ask a friend to look after some things for a while. If you don't miss these items, ask the friend to throw them out (or keep them if he or she wants to, of course).

● Don't let things build up so badly ever again. Keep four strong boxes marked Recycling/Charity Shop, Repairs/Alterations, Things to Sort Out, and The Dump. Keep the boxes where you can get at them easily – and then don't forget to use them.

● If the mess belongs to someone you live or work with, negotiate with them. They probably have a different set of priorities to you, so be patient. Explain to them what a calm environment means to you, in terms of feeling in control, and, above all, simplifying your life.

DIRECT ACTION

● Invest in a digital camera that links to your computer. At a stroke you will get rid of the need for photo albums and endless reams of photos you don't really like.

● Don't shuffle mess around from place to place. Pick up an object – any object. Do you like it? Is it in the right place? Does it need fixing before you can use it? What precisely are you going to do with it? Whatever you do, don't put it down somewhere else – deal with it now. There, that's one less item to think about!

● Use color and lighting to improve the situation. A well thought-out color scheme can reduce the sense of clutter. Rationalize and regroup objects by type, color, shape, or texture. If you have ten objects in varying shades of one color, they will look better together than scattered around. Lighting can create pools of calm, and make areas that you wish to play down less obvious. Use spotlights, concealed lights, uplights, and candles for different effects.

INSTANT CLUTTER-BUSTERS

De-junking is a habit as much as a discipline:

● Never add to the junk – just subtract from it.

● Ask mail-order firms to take your name off their lists.

● Put some work into making things attractive in the first place, so it's easier to keep them that way.

● Gain the agreement of those you live with that you will all pull together on keeping things in order.

the home workout

If you don't have time to get to the gym, or lack the resolve to jog with the dog, there is another option. Research is telling us that all those boring domestic chores that we have always tried to avoid have a big bonus – they keep us fit. It seems that our grandparents, who had much lower rates of diabetes, heart disease, and other ailments that are linked to low levels of exercise, automatically got a workout by doing the household chores. They also walked and did other forms of manual work more often than we do. Our laborsaving household appliances and convenience-based lifestyles are doing us no favors at all.

Sitting in front of the television you burn up about 100 calories an hour and your metabolism is barely above resting level. If you iron while you watch TV, you automatically increase the calories you use by 40 percent. More vigorous activities such as vacuuming, gardening, or washing the car will kick-start your metabolism to work at a faster pace for a few hours afterward. Shown opposite are some of the benefits you get from everyday chores.

When you carry out any tasks, maximize their value by stretching a little farther (you could put things on top shelves) or by increasing the activity (say, running up the stairs instead of walking). Even times of rest are opportunities to work out – with isometric exercises. Even a rocking chair used regularly will work the quadriceps muscles (at the fronts of the thighs) enough to improve their shape over the period of a year.

ACTIVITY	CALORIES BURNED	HEALTH BENEFITS
Carrying your shopping home	200 per half hour	Similar to using weights in the gym, particularly if you stop periodically, bend with knees keeping back straight, and pick up the bags again. Keep weight evenly distributed between two loads to reduce strain on neck and back.
Digging the garden	320 per half hour	Good cardiovascular exercise. Uses the thigh and calf muscles. Be careful not to strain your back.
Weeding the garden	120 per half hour	Bending and straightening uses the thighs, but make sure you bend knees and use stomach muscles as well, to avoid straining your back. Squats give an even more intense workout and are less hard on your back.
Making beds	70 per quarter hour	Lots of bending, and possibly lifting activity.
Scrubbing the bath	100 per quarter hour	Works the triceps and biceps (upper arm muscles). Scrubbing stubborn stains works best.
Running up the stairs	270 per half hour	Cardiovascular workout. Take items up the stairs, at a run, several times a day for an equivalent to using the stair machine at the gym.
Ironing	70 per half hour	You are standing still, but if you work your arm muscles by pressing down, you can increase the benefits. Change hands to work both arms.
Vacuuming	100 per half hour	Arms get a workout by pushing and pulling. Work up a sweat by vacuuming the whole house at one time.
Washing the car	150 per half hour	Uses your arm and abdominal muscles. Increase the stretch over the roof and into difficult corners.
Painting and decorating	350 per hour	Maximize your stretch up into nooks and crannies. Decorating uses your biceps and triceps.

harmonious
workspaces

Whatever your most time-consuming activity is – work, parenting, job-seeking, looking after the home, or even being a person of leisure, you can do it better if your environment is harmonious, satisfying, and enjoyable. Whether you are based primarily at home, in an office, on the road, or in another place, maximize your productivity and your sense of wellbeing by following these simple guiding principles.

CREATE A HARMONIOUS ENVIRONMENT

A few quick and simple fixes will make sure your workplace is a joyful, comfortable, and pleasing environment. Taking time out regularly to declutter your workspace can help you to reorganize your priorities and get to grips with exactly where you are in your planning. Schedule regular tidying sessions, say once a week. At the end of these you will feel much better in general, and clearer about your priorities. Fill (and then empty) your wastebasket with all unnecessary papers and notes; clear away pencils and paperclips; keep filing up to date; go through your in-tray and clear it. Whether your workplace is an office or the cab of a truck, a school or a factory, the same principles apply.

STRESS-FREE LIVING POINTS 51–55

❍ Fill an empty desk space with a vase of fresh flowers, a framed photo, or a bowl of fruit.

❍ Use color to create calm or just to please the eye. If your desk is covered with mismatched junk, perhaps you could invest in pleasing desk accessories and an attractive cushion for your chair. Ensure that the lighting in your workspace is kind to your eyes.

❍ Make sure that your chair is comfortable and at the right height and that the angle of your computer screen doesn't cause neck strain.

❍ A harmonious workspace is also dependent upon having an easy relationship with your work colleagues, people you do business with, and any others you come into contact with. A key tip: remember to say please and thank you.

❍ Good clear communication is easy when you focus on it. Listen to others and empathize if need be. Then say exactly what you mean in a way that is not challenging or offensive to other people.

SEEK BALANCE

An imbalance between work and personal life is a common source of discontent, but there are some simple ways to improve this situation:

● Creating a cutoff at the end of the working day makes it easier to stick to the stopping time you have set, and helps you leave your work worries behind. A cutoff that works well for some is to go to the gym at the end of the day.
● Acknowledge that you need time to recharge your batteries, and don't feel guilty about relaxing.
● Create time for your family and friends. We can have many jobs in a lifetime, but usually only a handful of close friends and family — so nurture and appreciate these relationships.
● Include your family in planning and share your successes and daily thoughts to make them feel included. Make a point of staying tuned in to their needs and discussing those as well as your own.

STRESS-FREE LIVING POINTS 56–60

○ To control work pressure, learn to delegate some of the work.

○ When you take on a job, be realistic about how much time you really need and have.

○ Take a few moments to prioritize, aim not to spend too much time on irrelevancies.

○ Approach a job in the simplest way. Break down large tasks into manageable chunks.

○ Take time out to review and plan.

LOOK AFTER YOUR NEEDS

You are (probably) not superhuman. If you find that you are doing it all — working long hours and then coming home and cooking, cleaning, putting the kids to bed, etc. — and smiling all the while (while inside feeling resentful), something is likely to give eventually. Stop doing it all yourself, rope in colleagues, friends and family, and delegate.

Many people fall for the idea that they need to work harder and harder if they are to achieve results. Really effective people, however, have honed their organizational and problem-solving skills and quite often do not even break into a sweat!

Planning and prioritizing are specific skills that can be developed with practice and will provide rewards many times greater than the time you've invested. To begin, all you need is a piece of paper, a pen, and an hour of time. Focus on whatever aspect you want to do something about and you will find inspirations you didn't know you had in you. For more about prioritizing, see "Learn to value yourself" (pages 86–7).
● Take a break from time to time during the working day to switch tasks, move around a bit, and clear your mind. Often your priorities, or the solutions to problems, suddenly become clear as a result.
● Don't feel that to please others you need to be seen to be working hard. You can't possibly please everyone all the time. Remind them, and yourself, that the results are what's important and how you get them is up to you. This way you make your immediate needs a priority.

Enjoy your work — you spend a lot of time at this activity so it might as well inspire and motivate you. Ask yourself:
● What are my aims and goals?
● What aspect of my work really pleases me?
● How can I get more of this into my day?
● How can I develop a more positive outlook?
● What is there to learn about my job that will keep me motivated and inspired?

HOME TRUTHS

Taking a moment to stop and think about your priorities at home can give you a better place to live. Choices include:

- A warm and welcoming kitchen
- A personal retreat
- A sexy bedroom
- A bathroom you can luxuriate in
- An elegant living room
- A separate television area
- A comfortable space for guests to stay
- A place where everyone can work

color boosts

The colors around you can have an effect on your wellbeing in all sorts of ways. Some colors can enhance your feelings of happiness, some can help to calm you, making you quiet and peaceful, and others can invigorate you and boost energy levels.

According to color therapists, the psychological effects of color are connected to the energy of different colors and their different wavelengths and rates of vibration. Science has determined that there might be an instinctive survival mechanism involved. For instance, we perceive blue and green – the colors of water, forests, and plants, from which we derive sustenance – as relaxing, and we feel safe with them. Blue, violet, and turquoise are also the colors that promote the brain waves that accompany relaxation. Red, the color of fire, provokes excitement and even anxiety and can raise blood pressure.

When you are moving into a new home, or thinking of redecorating part of your home, is the perfect time to evaluate how you feel about color and how you can bring its enhancing effects into your life. Do you want your home to feel cozy, nurturing, peaceful, light, spacious, calming, or energetic – or all of these?

Start by figuring out which colors really resonate with you. Which are the palettes you particularly enjoy? Which are you naturally drawn to? If you were to be given an imaginary color massage or you could bathe in color, which ones would you choose?

AROUND THE HOUSE

● First decide on a color scheme. If your place is small it may be better to stick to one palette throughout. If it is larger you can probably go for more variation.

● Make up a board of color swatches and paint splashes, as interior decorators do. Visit the decorating section of a department store to pick up tips on using color.

● If you want to learn more about how colors complement each other, take a short course on interior design, painting, or color therapy.

● Make a decision about whether you are going to use neutrals or brights, patterns or plains – or a mixture.

● Be wary of high-fashion colors that will quickly date. On the other hand, if you make thoughtful choices, you can create classics of which you never tire.

● Have confidence in your own style – this is your individuality and your personality. Learn from those who know about combining colors and who will stop you making expensive mistakes – then adopt their advice.

● Continue your color preferences through to your wardrobe, car, office, desk, and yard.

STRESS-FREE LIVING POINTS 61–65

❍ Once you have chosen the color you need (see below), several simple color therapy techniques will help you achieve peace and relaxation. The first and best-known technique is very easy: gaze at a board painted with your chosen color until you feel its vibrations healing you.

❍ Visualize the chosen color, then meditate on it.

❍ Add skin-safe coloring to your bathwater and immerse yourself in it for 10–15 minutes.

❍ Color the water in a vase and let it filter sunlight into the room. You can also use stained glass to create colored light.

❍ In the mornings, pick a boosting color to energize your mood.

COLOR ASSOCIATIONS

Purple/violet — These have been used to calm people with mental disorders and are linked to creative impulses.

Red — Red is associated with vitality and overcoming negative thoughts. Too much can make us uncomfortable.

Orange — Connected with joyousness and the releasing of emotions, orange is a good antidepressant.

Yellow — Happy and uplifting, yellow aids the power of discrimination and stimulates new ideas.

Green — Green, the color of nature, eases stress and emotional trauma, though lime and olive can be detrimental.

Blue — Blue inspires mental control, clarity, and creativity and is calming.

Indigo — Invigorating, but too much dark blue, however, can be depressing.

a nurturing
place

Eating for health and vitality is something we all know we need to do to maximize our energy levels and to avoid illness. But accomplishing this is another matter, particularly if the way you use your kitchen makes healthy eating hard work. Simplify your kitchen and your use of it, and you'll find that healthier eating follows automatically.

FOCUS ON FOOD – It is wonderful if your kitchen is the heart of your home. However, allowing it to become a repository for all the clutter of life, from piles of mail and paperwork to children's toys, discarded shoes, and ironing, will make it difficult to focus on the main purpose of this room – nurturing your health and relationship with delicious, wholesome food.

MAKE A LIST – Keep a current list of staples you are getting low on, and take the list to the stores with you.

AVOID TEMPTATION – Don't buy ingredients for really complicated dishes that you know you will probably never get around to making.

WEEKLY MENU PLAN – Take time once a week to make a menu plan. This means it will be easier to stop yourself from buying lots of unnecessary food that ends up going to waste. Check that for maximum nutritional benefit your menu plan includes a couple of fish meals and about three vegetarian choices a week.

HEAD OFF HUNGER – Make fridge-grazing work for you. If you are in the habit of fridge-grazing when hunger strikes, prepare for this by buying lots of healthy quick dips and snacks. These could include olives, pickles, crudités, dried fruit compote (soak in black tea or fruit tea to serve), hummus, salsa, fish paté, or cottage cheese.

STOCK UP – Take advantage of quieter times in your week to "feed" your freezer with nutrition-packed meals such as ratatouille, pasta sauces, and vege-chillis.

ENJOY YOURSELF – If there's room in your kitchen for people to eat, and to sit and chat, then you can enjoy cooking with friends. It becomes a form of entertainment if you are relaxed, happy, and enjoying each other's company. Everyone can pitch in and help with the peeling, chopping, and stirring.

KEEP IT SIMPLE – Get into the habit of wok-cooking, steam-frying, and making one-pot meals and huge main-meal salads. The idea is to minimize clearing up. Get your guests to keep their silverware from course to course, French style. Even better, serve sensuous finger food and then mop up the juices with bread.

A ZEN FRIDGE – Is your fridge a jumble of unidentifiable foods and jars past their expiration dates? Or even worse, a food-desert containing nothing but chocolate and beer? Take the time once a month to create a refrigerator that is ordered and neat, with perishables clearly visible so that they can be eaten first.

A HEALTHY FRIDGE – A good way to do an instant health audit on your fridge is to see whether at least one third of the contents are fresh fruit and vegetables.

time to eat

Healthy eating maximizes energy levels and guards against illness. Start with the basics – shopping – and you will have all the time you need to eat well.

In the hurly-burly of life, it may seem that you barely have time to eat, let alone time to eat healthily. But it is even more important to eat well if you are busy and pressured. Your body needs first-class fuel to get you through the challenges of the day. If you barely have time even to think about this, the following ideas should help you simplify your food preparation so that you always have something nutritious on hand.

HEALTHY PANTRY STANDBYS

When you are tired or have unexpected guests, prepare a healthy fast meal such as Spanish omelet; tortillas stuffed with Mediterranean vegetable salad; pasta with an anchovy, olive, and tomato sauce; three-bean salad with crusty bread; poached eggs on a bed of garlicky spinach; wild mushroom risotto; or broiled (grilled) polenta with sun-dried tomatoes and herb and Parmesan topping. To produce healthy and nourishing meals like these in 20 minutes, keep the following in your pantry at all times:

● Canned, bottled, or vacuum-packed tomatoes, legumes (pulses), olives, sun-dried tomatoes, anchovies, tuna, tortillas, olive oil, and balsamic vinegar.

● Dried goods: rice, pasta (a variety of shapes), dried wild mushrooms, couscous, thin rye biscuits.
● Fresh foods: potatoes, onions, garlic, eggs, Parmesan.

HEALTHY FREEZER STANDBYS

When you are inspired to cook or bake, make best use of your freezer by cooking triple quantities. Stock up on portion-sized freezer containers and label each item with name, date, and serving details if relevant. Just remember to defrost your choice in time. Use your freezer as a complement to your pantry, and aim to keep the following items in it:

● Milk (for emergencies).
● Breads (different varieties and grains).
● A variety of vegetables. Picked at their peak, frozen vegetables often have more nutrients in them than "fresh" vegetables that have been transported, stored, and displayed for longer than is ideal. Stock up on chopped spinach, chopped bell peppers, baby carrots, corn, beans, and peas.
● Dips like hummus and salsa freeze well.
● Fish is an ideal freezer food. Deep-frozen fresh sardines are a real treat when defrosted and broiled (grilled).
● Fresh soups – homemade or store-bought.

STRESS-FREE LIVING POINTS 66–71

❍ Planning your meals means you can avoid being faced with messy cooking jobs and messier kitchens, reduce the food bills, and have plenty of nutritious leftovers. For example, cook a batch of beans. Freeze some for later use, and divide the rest into three portions – use one for a casserole that evening; purée another portion with garlic, tahini, olive oil, yogurt, and/or lemon for a dip; and add the final one to a salad or soup for work the next day.

❍ For an even simpler option, poach some salmon for 10–15 minutes for your evening meal, leaving plenty for a meal the next day – it is twice as delicious cold in sandwiches or salads.

❍ Chicken is always versatile. Roast one for a main meal, then use the leftovers for a chicken salad or stuffed pita bread to take to work the next day, and use the carcass for delicious chicken-noodle soup.

❍ When you buy your fresh vegetables once or twice a week, wash and scrub those that are dirty, wash salad leaves, spin them dry, and store them in bags in the fridge – then, when it comes to cooking healthy meals, you won't be put off by lengthy preparation.

❍ In the morning, cut up a selection of crudités, seal them in an airtight box in the fridge, and snack on them throughout the day.

❍ Keep leftover red wine for tasty, fat-free cooking – it is rich in antioxidants as well. Freeze it in ice-cube trays for handy amounts that will give a lift to sauces and stews.

HEALTHY TAKE-OUTS

If you don't feel like cooking, you can get a take-out and still eat healthily. Here are some good choices:

● Italian food can be great as long as you stick to tomato or wine sauces instead of thick cheese or white sauces.

● Order your pizza with a little less cheese and double the tomato, herbs, and vegetables. Accompany it with a side order of salad.

● For a Chinese take-out, opt for boiled rice instead of fried, choose stir-fried instead of sweet-and-sour, and have steamed dim sum instead of fried spring rolls. Soups are usually another good bet.

● Indian food can be high in fat. However, anything from the tandoori oven will be low-fat, and plain rice with some of the vegetable choices such as chickpea curry or sag bhaji is positively saintly if the vegetables are not drowned in oil.

● All Japanese food fits the bill as it is low-fat yet tasty. Go easy on the soy sauce, though. Enjoy sushi, sashimi, or teriyaki. Even tempura is not as greasy as fried foods of other cuisines.

ADD THESE ITEMS TO YOUR SHOPPING BASKET

The most inspiring places to shop are at your local farmers' market or at small specialty shops, where there are countless fabulous new taste experiences awaiting you. Failing this, get to know the position of healthy foods on the supermarket shelves so that you can shop "on automatic" and still keep healthy by avoiding junk foods.

● Shelled fresh nuts and seeds, kept in sealed jars in the fridge, are great for healthy snacks rich in essential fats.

● All vegetables are healthy. Some that you may not have thought about include artichokes and asparagus, which are great as appetizers and have liver- and kidney-detoxifying properties. Beansprouts are easy for salads and sandwiches and are rich in beta-carotene and folic acid. Tomatoes and watermelon are rich in lycopene, which fights breast and prostate cancers and keeps eyes healthy. Broccoli and cauliflower, good for crudités with dips, are rich in vitamin C and are potent anti-cancer foods.

● Rye crackers, and rice cakes make healthy alternatives to wheat-based breads and crackers, particularly if you are avoiding wheat, and many flavors are now available.

● Buy cold-pressed oils in small quantities and keep them in your fridge to prevent these valuable essential fats from going rancid.

● Use yogurt for making creamy sauces to serve with main meals, as well as for creamy desserts, or just to eat with fruit as a snack.

DELECTABLE WORK-TIME LUNCHES

When you are under pressure at work, it is easy to forget to eat well, but you need a midday break to recharge your batteries, and nourishing food will enhance your energy for the afternoon stretch.

● Always eat a piece of fruit and a portion of vegetables with your lunch to add to the general nutritional value of the meal and ensure that you get your minimum of five portions a day. For instance, you could have a couple of tomatoes, a handful of carrot sticks or olives, a cup of vegetable or bean soup, or a glass of vegetable juice.

● The healthiest take-out lunches are sandwiches made with wholewheat (wholegrain) bread, tortillas filled with salad ingredients, a salad box (avoid those with too much mayonnaise or other dressing), a sushi box, a baked potato stuffed with tuna or baked beans, or vegetable soup. The deli counter at a nearby supermarket is also certain to yield some delicious options.

● Keep wholewheat crackers, or rice cakes in your desk drawer and bring whatever you have at home to add to them – hard-boiled eggs, canned fish, hummus, chicken, lean meat, or bean salad.

create more leisure

There are only 24 hours in each day. How you use those hours makes the difference between feeling happy, relaxed, and fulfilled at the end of each day or feeling that you are on a treadmill and can't get off. For many of us, time is the greatest luxury of all. So how do you squeeze more time out of your 24 hours? You don't. What you do is make sure that time to do what you want is treated as the valuable commodity it is and is moved higher up your priority list. You need to plan around this list in the course of a busy life. This is how to plan your escape:

● Get your calendar or day-planner out now – really do this right now – and make your relaxation plans. If you do not get enough rest, you will not recharge your batteries and you will be less effective. Spare time will always remain elusive if you don't plan for it. It must be this way round rather than the other way round – working until you are finished and then taking time out never works.

● In your calendar or day-planner, note all your free weekends and what you want to do with them. Strike a balance between rest and recreation. Avoid exhausting yourself with lots of chores – get them out of the way on a half-day and spend the remaining 1½ days relaxing and doing things that you really want to do. If you don't do this you may find that the year goes by without your having done anything inspiring.

● Also in your calendar or day-planner, enter your full vacation entitlement for each year, and highlight long holiday weekends as well. If you aren't taking your full vacation entitlement each year, ask yourself why. Are you really a workaholic and do you not have any other things you want to do, or are you just a little disorganized? Aren't there any colleagues who can take over from you while you are away? Find solutions to these questions.

● If you are a chronic overworker, go so far as to mark hours in the day or evening when you can relax some of the time. Making an appointment for daily time out may be the only way forward. However you do it, it's essential to build "me-time" into the day, as it will increase your sense of control and wellbeing.

● If you cannot afford vacations, work out a way to finance them or plan for an at-home break. At-home vacations may involve switching off the phone and making the time to do something like replanning your environment. This can be highly satisfying as long as you include some leisure activities such as sleeping late and eating out. Funding away-from-home vacations is easier if you visit friends or do a home swap for a week or so.

● Figure out what the time pressures are in your life, and grade them in importance by allocating a number from 1 to 5 to each of them. Devise solutions by writing out lists of pros and cons. Work a step at a time in order to avoid being overwhelmed and giving yourself yet more to do.

● If you are the sort of person who can always find one more job to do, you probably find it difficult to relax. But if you aren't careful, you will carry on until you drop. Learn to create cutoff times, and remember those scheduled rest periods you put on your calendar or in your day-planner.

● Share responsibilities. Find someone with whom you can share delivering the kids to school, babysitting, brainstorming sessions, or warehouse shopping trips (take turns and divide the purchases in half).

● Remember, there is nothing so powerful as taking action. If you didn't get your calendar or day-planner out at the first suggestion, get it out now!

your

RELATION

10 steps to
domestic bliss

Home is ideally a refuge, a place where you can be yourself and relax. However, if tensions mount between yourself and your partner, or any of the other people you live with, then it is no longer a sanctuary. Learning to cherish and nurture each other through good times and bad is the foundation of rewarding relationships.

1 Acknowledge your partner's successes. You can help to build the other person's self-esteem – and, at any rate, you know how nice it is to receive a compliment. Encourage and help your partner in his or her dreams. If you don't agree with their ideas, give solid reasons and avoid being scornful or ridiculing ideas. If you are finding it difficult to be supportive it could well be that on some level you are feeling threatened – examine your feelings and work out what you find difficult about your partner's success. Support your partner emotionally through good and bad times.

2 Recognize different needs. Some absolute basics make life easier in a relationship, and taking care of practicalities can help prolong romance. Maybe separate bathrooms would help, or different eating arrangements, or even separate vacations. Perhaps it needs to be a priority to make the shed in the backyard into a den without further disagreement. If your partner is really no good at getting up in the morning but is lively in the evening, or vice versa, take this into account when sharing out the chores, instead of getting irritated all the time.

SHIPS

Just trust yourself, then you will know how to live.

3 Honesty is the best policy. Keeping secrets from your partner about yourself is fairly similar to lying, and there is rarely a place for lying in a relationship. In the end, secrets can lead to further lies, and then discovery and disillusionment. If there is something about your past that you are holding back, perhaps for fear of your partner's reaction, you are not committing yourself to the relationship whole-heartedly. If your partner cannot accept  something about you, then the foundation of your relationship is something to work on. Learning to love and respect the other person, with all his or her faults and failings, as he or she must love and respect you with all your faults and failings, is the most likely path to a successful relationship.

4 Put some effort into building relationships with your partner's family and friends. This can help you under-stand your partner's background and the part that the family plays in your partner's life, as well as giving you some insights into his or her personality and interests. Of course, your own background will also color your view of family relationships, and imposing those interpretations on your partner's family behavior may be a reason for different behavior patterns. It is not always easy to acknowledge that, when you enter into a relationship, you also enter a relationship on one level or another with your loved one's family, past, and friends. In addition, it is important to realize that we all get different things from various relationships and that rarely can one person fill all roles. If you feel threatened, stifled, or distanced, by your partner's friendships, examine why this is the case and discuss what can be done about it. Accepting your partner's friends and family (even if you don't involve yourself with them), whatever the circumstances, sends signals that you trust the other person's judgment and integrity.

5 It is easy to mistake physical closeness for emotional intimacy, especially early in a relationship. This can make the other person nervous. Intimacy is a goal for many people, but other people will settle for a version of love that suits their needs, such as companionship or shared material or social goals. Understanding which categories you and your partner fall into allows for a more honest view of the relationship. This is often easier after the initial excitement of the relationship has subsided a little.

6 Give comfort. When one of you is feeling low, spend time together quietly just to offer comfort. With busy lives it is easy to go in different directions, and your time together is something that may need to be consciously created. But don't stifle each other — get the balance right for you both.

7 Establish your personal attitudes to sex early on. If one of you has a casual attitude to sex and the other doesn't, then you are heading for rocky patches later on. Rarely do people have consistent sex drives, and changes in sexual relationships can leave the partners feeling insecure and rejected. Ironically, there can be much difficulty in talking frankly about sexual issues, the most intimate and shared acts within a relationship, and there are lots of presuppositions about performance, ego, and satisfaction. It may be difficult initially, but being able to talk about sex will help avoid major areas of misunderstanding.

8 Listen intently to your partner so you can hear the real message behind what is actually being said. Do not always attempt to impose your own beliefs – in other words, do not over-interpret – but search for what the other person may be finding hard to put into words. Help them to explore their sentiments farther with tactful questions. Listening is a tremendous skill and takes practice, time, and patience. It is probably the single most important thing, after respect and trust, that helps to build solid relationships that really last.

9 Make a real commitment to staying in touch when you are apart. Being thoughtful comes naturally at the beginning of a relationship but often wanes later on. Instead of assuming that everything is all right with your partner, be considerate, and this means staying in touch when apart. Small things can keep the flame of romance alive and make the other person feel appreciated. These include knowing their likes and dislikes and showing you do in thoughtful acts. Get some movie or theater tickets as a surprise; organize a babysitter so you can spend time together; bring back a special food the other person really enjoys; and pay genuine compliments at every opportunity. Your partner will feel special and cherished.

10 Accept the differences in viewpoints between the two sexes. This is a rich vein for comedy but in truth is a serious point. Sociological conditioning and hormonal effects mean that even those who are most ardent about equality agree that there are three typical viewpoints – the female, the male, and the unisex. The issues include some that are seemingly less important such as shopping – sociologists tell us that men tend to be faster decision-makers and spend less time worrying about choices of, say, kitchen-unit design than women. There are also more important and divisive issues, such as those of nest-building and starting families, which are generally more pressing issues for women. Then there are questions of communication, with typical male and female patterns of expression and comprehension. Instead of getting frustrated with each other, perhaps this is a time to shrug your shoulders and say, "Vive la différence" and to embrace the differences instead of fighting them.

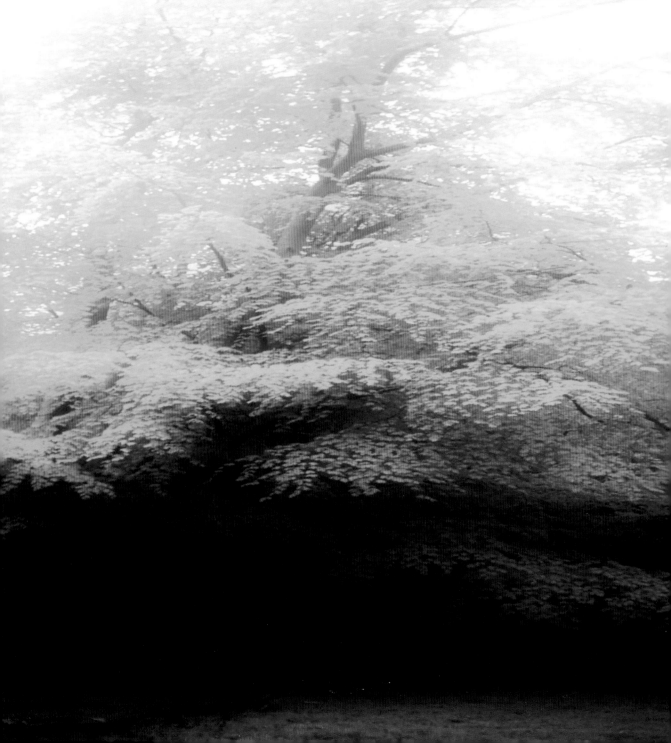

instant unwind

WHY YOU NEED IT

Very few relationships thrive on constant togetherness, or, even more intense, on constant neediness. Being with the other person can obviously be a joy and a pleasure, but most relationships will grow and thrive if the people in that relationship also have time to themselves – to reflect, to have space and peace, to pursue their own activities, and, yes, to be selfish.

There will always be times when you need to retreat; being a considerate human being can wear thin if you don't get time out. Your home will be a lot happier if you are able to relax when you need to.

Downtime is particularly necessary if you are a caregiver. If you look after small children, an elderly relative, or an invalid, or you play a supporting role in your partner's business and domestic life, you need time out to recharge your batteries.

Relationships where both partners are at home all the time need especially careful planning and a generous spirit to avoid daily irritations building up. One way to achieve this is to agree that you each have your own areas of responsibility, where you don't step on each other's toes all the time, and also your own agendas for time out.

Downtime is time to yourself to do precisely what you would like to do. You may choose to do something active or creative, but this is not a time to catch up with work.

Relaxing during downtime is high on most people's list. Yet for many, relaxing is easier said than done. Therapeutic relaxation is quite another thing to going out for a drink at a bar, or a workout at the gym. If you really need to relax mind and body, do a specific relaxation exercise of your choice.

STRESS-FREE LIVING POINTS 77–83

❍ True relaxation does take practice. Ideally you need to set aside 15–20 minutes twice a day to clear your mind and relax in a calm setting. Many relaxation techniques, such as yoga (see pages 14–17), are actually improved with the help of a partner.

❍ Tried and tested self-relaxation techniques include hypnosis, yoga, meditation (see pages 18–19), autogenic training, t'ai chi, biofeedback, color therapy (see pages 68–9), and flotation therapy.

❍ Find a space (in your bedroom, den, office, or yard) and make it clear to the rest of the household that it is out of bounds for, say, the next hour. In this time, do some relaxation exercises, read a book, draw – anything but your usual activities.

❍ Don't watch the television during this time. Even watching a movie is not the same as taking time out to relax. There's a difference between escapism and relaxation. There certainly is a place for enjoying a good movie, particularly a comedy, but the best way to relax is through relaxation.

❍ Be firm, but realize that it takes time to "train" others in your household. Eventually everyone in the house will realize that relaxation time is special time.

❍ Respect others' need for time and space. Recognize that other people need their time to relax too, and that during others' downtime it is only fair not to interrupt them.

❍ Just as children need play time, so do adults. Make sure everyone in the family has relaxation time.

quick-fix tips for a
happy home

According to researchers, small daily hassles cause at least as much stress as the big things in life. The major culprits are constant, steady tensions in relationships.

You know how easy it is for tensions to build up. You always like to get 10 hours of beauty sleep, while your partner likes to read until midnight… The grandparents "treat" the children with bags of candy while you've been aiming to get them off junk food… Your partner wants you to have dinner at the table so that you can share some quality time, but you want to eat in front of the television and wind down without the small talk… We all have different needs, and accommodating them is the best way to iron out tensions, even if it seems difficult initially.

PROBLEM: I just don't feel appreciated at home.
ANSWER: Do nice things for the people in your life – your partner, roommate, in-laws, and others. Small kindnesses build into an atmosphere of appreciation. Give someone a sprig of flowers, record your partner's favorite television show, make a special meal for your family. You will quickly find these kindnesses reciprocated.

PROBLEM: My partner is really tight with money and I just want to live a little.
ANSWER: People's attitudes to money are shaped by their history, and different views on finances are a major cause of discontent in relationships. Money can be used as a form of control, while some partners are free-spending to the point where they can cause financial problems. If you have radically different spending patterns, it may be best to have three bank accounts – one for each partner and one for the household.

PROBLEM: We don't get time together very often.
ANSWER: Go halves or even quarters on your time allowances. Mutually agree that if your partner wants to vegetate in front of the television, that's fine, as long as you get two evenings a week together when you do something special. In this busy world, couples and families sometimes even have to schedule their time together.

PROBLEM: When parents, in-laws, or neighbors visit, they tend to take over or be nosy.
ANSWER: Be welcoming and instead of getting up-tight when they transgress your beliefs about how guests should behave, offer positive suggestions. Don't wail privately that they never offer to do the dishes, but say, "If I wash and you dry, we can have more time to… [play with the kids, go for a walk, watch the TV show]." Very few guests will refuse a direct request. In the meantime, learn to say no, firmly but kindly, espe-cially in your own home.

PROBLEM: Nobody ever agrees in this household.
ANSWER: Make a habit of finding common ground, and don't look for differences. The agreement of both people is not always essen-tial, though it helps. You can be the one to instigate the circumstances where you look for answers, and can be the one who thinks carefully about the issues. Keep the channels of communication open, and avoid laying down the law, but be firm and clear about your own needs.

PROBLEM: We always have the same old arguments, like a broken record.
ANSWER: It is easy to get stuck in repetitive rows. Ask yourself: are these rows about the real issues? Find the bigger issue and address it. For instance, if you are cross about your partner going for a drink after work, the real reason for your anger might be the fact that you never get to go out yourself, or that you need help with the children so you can pursue your own activities. Instead of criticiz-ing, try an explanation: "I am unhappy about… because…" Then move on to proposing your solution: "Next week, can we do…?"

learn to
value yourself

If life seems an uphill battle it might be that you are aspiring to perform in areas that do not really suit you, or trying to accommodate relationships that don't fit your value system, while denying yourself the pleasures of doing things you prefer and being with people to whom you are really suited.

YOUR PERSONAL VALUE SYSTEM

Ask yourself the following questions and write down the answers in a notebook. There may be several answers to each question, in which case put them in order of importance (you could grade them from 1 to 4):

● What do I feel about friendship?
● What do I think about honesty?
● When am I willing to give?
● When do I need to receive?

Answering these questions will allow you to re-evaluate your relationships at times of change or crisis. By crystalizing these thoughts, you are automatically better placed to decide if they have served you well in the past. If they have not, then you know you need to change your value system. Understanding your personal value system will help you to seek out those who are in tune with your own sentiments.

WHAT ARE YOUR DRIVERS?

Ask yourself the following questions and write down the answers in a notebook. Review your answers every so often as they may change, mature, or even surprise you pleasantly by coming to fruition. If you are more content, your home and work relationships will be happier ones.

● What do I feel passionate about?
● What or who inspires me?
● What are my strengths?
● What motivates me?
● What do I want to do more of?

All the above questions are framed in positive terms. This is important, as so often we are perfectly aware of what we do not want, while being oblivious to what we really do need or want. Asking yourself, "What do I want to do less of?" or, "What do I hate least of all?" is a paralyzing way of viewing a situation. Turn your communication with yourself around to express things in positive terms and you will begin to find answers.

YOUR PERSONAL JIGSAW

Make a three-square by three-square grid. Label each of these nine squares with a major aspect of your life, such as family, work, sport, leisure, hobby, spiritual, social, romantic relationship, partner, family, friends, time out, personal development, adventure, addiction, food, wellness/illness. These are only examples – your grid will probably be completely different to those of other people. Now decide which elements dominate your life and which ones you would like to give more time to. If work, for instance, dominates your life, then two things can happen: (1) The other areas diminish in significance and you don't have time for a more rounded life. (2) If your work lets you down in some way, it may seem as if your whole world falls apart because you don't attach enough value to other aspects to balance out the effect. If your grid is balanced, your life is likely to be content.

STRESS-FREE LIVING POINTS 84–88

○ Knowing yourself is the first step to loving yourself. A few moments a day spent considering your aims and goals could change the course of your life.

○ Know your inner drives, and make time for what you are passionate about.

○ Value those who value you.

○ Balance all the elements in your life and you will find relaxation more readily.

○ Acknowledge your own achievements day by day.

Learning to communicate with yourself and give yourself an easier ride could be essential in helping you to work to your strengths. Negative thoughts are one of the most disempowering ways that we trip ourselves up. Here are some examples of self-destructive thought patterns:

PROBLEM: I'm not sure I'm getting anywhere with any of my goals and aims. How do I continue?
ANSWER: Celebrate your successes, no matter how small. If you don't mark your achievements, then they are devalued and you will barely notice them. Recognizing your achievements helps to build self-confidence, pride, and motivation.

PROBLEM: Every time I get near my goals, the rug seems to get pulled from under my feet, and all my work is lost.
ANSWER: Embrace change, rather than fearing it. Those who are inflexible are left stranded when plans do not go as expected, whereas those who can accept altered plans tend to bounce back and forge on.

PROBLEM: There is a limit to how hard I can work, and I feel that the demands on my time, from work, the family, and my own needs, are becoming overwhelming.
ANSWER: You don't need to work harder, just more effectively. By planning, thinking about problems, asking for help, and delegating, you can increase your output without working harder.

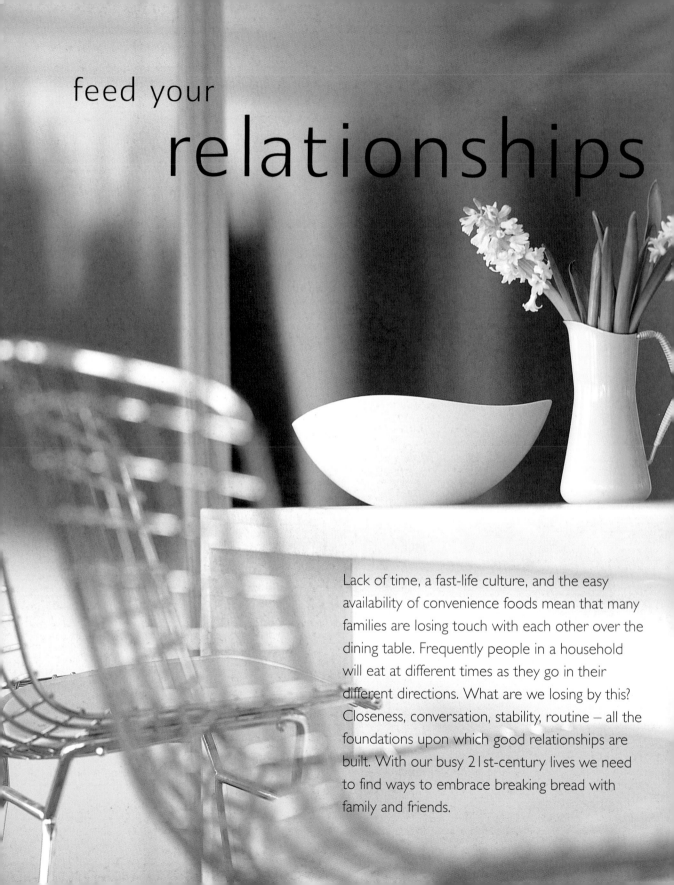

feed your
relationships

Lack of time, a fast-life culture, and the easy availability of convenience foods mean that many families are losing touch with each other over the dining table. Frequently people in a household will eat at different times as they go in their different directions. What are we losing by this? Closeness, conversation, stability, routine – all the foundations upon which good relationships are built. With our busy 21st-century lives we need to find ways to embrace breaking bread with family and friends.

Entertaining at home has taken a beating – which is hardly a surprise as the dinner party was obviously designed by a masochist. It certainly became popular at a time when households had easy access to domestic staff or stay-at-home housewives were the norm. Nobody ever said that it is workable to rush back from work, tidy the house like a whirling dervish, dress like a model, cook and serve a gourmet meal, and then clear up the mess afterward. It just doesn't make sense.

Indulge in some of these suggestions to make your life easier, your relationships warmer, and your entertaining easier and more enjoyable for everybody.

SLOWLY DOES IT

The Slow Food movement, started in Italy in 1989, urges us to return to a time when food was enjoyed and lingered over, when relationships could be built over regular family meals, when children learned from the kitchen and dining table, and when good, locally produced food was appreciated. This last principle supports local economies, preserves local specialties and customs, and cuts back on "food miles" (the distance food travels from source to mouth, which is adversely affecting our planet).

GOOD FRIENDS, GREAT FOOD

Entertaining friends at home is less formal these days. If space allows, center the occasion on the kitchen and choose meals where the cooking is part of the entertainment. Prepare dishes as your guests chop the final bits, while you all sip wine and chat.

● Prepare a stew in advance and bread dough in a machine. When your guests arrive, they can make the salad, while you put the stew on to heat up and bake the bread in the oven for ½–¾ hour. The warm aroma of baking bread will arouse everyone's appetites as they nibble on olives. Fresh fruit salad or dried fruit compote is the ideal finale.

● A main-meal salad is a good idea. Each person prepares one ingredient and in a short time you have a meal. You could include mixed salad leaves, chopped cooked chicken, halved seedless grapes, chopped nuts, halved cherry tomatoes, diagonally sliced green onions, and shaved Parmesan. Follow it with goat cheese and ripe peaches.

● Barbecues are a relaxed way to eat with friends. You could try seafood kabobs marinated with Thai flavors such as ginger and lemongrass; tandoori spiced chicken; or filleted leg of lamb marinated in balsamic vinegar and garlic.

STRESS-FREE LIVING POINTS 89–95

○ Taking a moment to add a bunch of flowers and selecting pretty plates and glasses turns any mealtime into a social occasion.

○ Treat meal preparation as a hobby to be enjoyed instead of a chore to be endured; use the time to chat and unwind.

○ Enjoy eating with friends and family.

○ Shop at farmers' markets or local stores.

○ Cook using local, seasonal produce.

○ Learn some traditional slow-cooking or speed-preparation tactics – many fine recipes are quick and easy to prepare.

○ Count how many fast food/convenience meals you eat during the week and aim to prepare fresh food for at least half of these meals in the future.

ROMANCE – THE FOOD OF LOVE

The dinner-date is the way that many romantic relationships begin. But as the relationship matures we often get chained to the kitchen microwave. Once upon a time perhaps you looked at your partner and were turned on as the juice from a squashy peach ran down in sensuous stickiness – now if this happens you may just think, "Ugh, what a mess…" What happened?

Rekindle passions by sharing ultra-romantic foodie sessions with your loved one on a regular basis. For instance, what is more romantic than shared finger food? A supremely sexy meal (which, though a little expensive, needs no preparation, meaning that you can spend more time making yourself delicious) could be a first course of oysters with lemon and Tabasco, or quail's eggs that you peel together and dip in celery salt; a main course of cold cooked lobster or giant cooked shrimps (prawns) with a dipping sauce, and prewashed salad leaves with dressing (yes, eat this too with your fingers); plus fabulous strawberries and dark liqueur chocolates for dessert. Even more romantic, light the candles, put on the music, and feed each other.

CHILD'S PLAY

Introduce your children to real food as soon as possible to help them develop a good relationship with it. Get them involved in food preparation – it may take longer and be quite messy, but they will enjoy all aspects – washing, chopping, mixing, stirring – and they love eating the results. Safety is always an issue, so make sure they are standing on a non-slip surface or sitting at the table. Help them with anything hot, and don't let them touch a pan of boiling water. They should not handle knives at all unless they are old enough to understand how to handle them safely.

● There are many simple dishes that children find easy to prepare and usually enjoy, including pasta, egg dishes, baked potatoes, sandwiches, and other staples such as sausages and beans. If you have a bread machine, make pizza dough to the uncooked-dough stage and it will keep in the fridge until dinnertime. Children love rolling it out on a baking sheet and sprinkling on lots of different toppings.

● Baking is often seen as suitable child's play, but children can have just as much fun washing and preparing vegetables and making main courses. They are more likely to eat a fish dish or a bean dish if they have been making it themselves. And you'll be amazed at how many raw vegetables they eat as they are chopping them.

● Buy a children's cookbook with big, bright pictures. If you have space, let your children grow some easy items in the garden (seed potatoes, radishes, and squash give satisfying results), or if space is at a premium, let them grow a few herbs in pots or some tomatoes in a small growing bag.

STRESS-FREE LIVING POINTS 96–101

❍ Easy meals can be the most mouthwatering. Finger food is romantic – try cold lobster or crab and dipping sauce, with hulled strawberries for dessert.

❍ Fondue is a simple treat for all the family. Vary the mix by using roasted vegetables and potato skins as dippers, and try fresh fruit slices, such as mango and papaya, dipped in chocolate sauce, for dessert.

❍ Barbecues minimize the domestic workload by allowing everyone to get involved.

❍ Allow children to experiment with cookery; they may enjoy doing the chores you don't like.

❍ Picky child eaters may be tempted more by their own cooking; encourage your child to experiment with vegetables and fish.

❍ Main-meal salads can be a healthy option for most people; just keep the dressings light.

rapid recipes for
lazy lunches

Sharing the conviviality of long, lazy lunches with friends and family is a real treat, particularly on weekends. Lunch parties are less formal than dinner parties, making for a more relaxed time, and you can wind down with good conversation afterward.

Lunch is a much undervalued meal. While the midday meal is still a major feature of Mediterranean cultures (with a siesta afterward) the sandwich has largely replaced it in the United States, Britain, and many other countries. Yet eating the main meal at midday and a light meal in the evening is much easier on the digestion. You could even offer "open house" on one or two Sundays each month and enjoy the spontaneity of friends dropping in – encourage them to bring a potluck contribution for everyone to enjoy.

SEASONAL EATING

Cooking in tune with the seasons makes a lazy lunch so much easier and more stylish. It is quite simple – you can create new recipes by combining your usual fare with the best seasonal produce. In this way you expand your repertoire effortlessly and manage to eat more healthily at the same time. So many recipes are adaptable to the seasons. If you make a filling Spanish omelet with a fresh tomato sauce and peasant bread in winter, substitute new potatoes, spinach, and sorrel in the summer and serve the omelet with a mixed leaf and herb salad. Pasta or risotto made with olive oil and garlic is the perfect foundation for new-season vegetables – add the first fava (broad) beans, baby fennel, bok choy, broccoli, or wild mushrooms.

In summer, add fresh peas, asparagus, baby zucchini (courgettes), cherries, or strawberries to your basket and create the taste of summer. In fall or winter, throw root vegetables, winter greens, squash, damson plums, or cranberries in the shopping cart and enjoy more comforting fare. By cooking in this way you will start to create new recipes with virtually no thought at all. Be relaxed about shopping, enjoy experimenting, and you won't look back.

FIVE-MINUTE SALMON CAKES

Serve these delicious and quick fish cakes with peeled fresh tomatoes blended in a blender into a coulis, and a green leaf and avocado salad with French dressing. All the minced/chopped ingredients can be put separately into a food processor and made in seconds, but take care not to overprocess to a paste. Serves 2.

6oz (170g) fish: 3oz (85g) salmon and 3oz (85g) firm white fish, minced, or fresh white crabmeat if you are feeling extravagant
4 green onions, trimmed and finely chopped
I small red bell pepper, de-seeded and finely chopped
I lime, half juiced and zest of whole lime grated
Handful of parsley, finely chopped
2 cups (100g) stale breadcrumbs (about 2 slices stale bread, crushed in blender)
Salt and pepper to taste
2–3 tbsp olive oil
Lime wedges, to garnish

Combine the fish, green onions, bell pepper, lime juice and zest, parsley, breadcrumbs, and seasoning in a bowl, and mix well with your hands. Form the mixture into four patties. Gently fry in the olive oil on a medium heat for about 3–4 minutes on each side (handle gently when turning the fish cakes over). Garnish with lime wedges.

BUCKWHEAT WITH ROAST BELL PEPPERS, CHICKPEAS, AND OLIVES

This is an ideal summer first course and can be prepared in advance. It is suitable for vegetarians and those on wheat-free regimen. Serves 4 as a first course or 2 as a main course.

2 red or yellow bell peppers or 5oz (150g) jar antipasto peppers
Olive oil
6½oz (180g) roasted buckwheat
3½ cups (750ml) stock or water
12 green olives, pitted and halved
15oz (425g) can chickpeas, drained
I lemon
¼ tsp paprika
½ tsp grated nutmeg
Salt and pepper to taste
Chopped parsley and toasted pine nuts or pumpkin seeds to garnish

If using raw bell peppers, roast in a pan in a medium-hot oven with a little olive oil for about 20–25 minutes until soft. Allow to cool. De-seed, but there's no need to peel. Cut the flesh into strips. If roasted buckwheat is not available, roast your own in a frying pan with a small amount of oil, stirring constantly until toasted and golden. Put the roasted buckwheat and the stock or water in a large pan, cover, and bring to the boil. Simmer for 15 minutes, or until all the liquid is absorbed. Remove from the heat and allow it to stand for a further 5 minutes. Place all the other ingredients apart from the garnish in a pan and warm through. Add the buckwheat and stir. Serve, garnished with the parsley and pine nuts or pumpkin seeds.

ROAST TOMATO AND GOAT CHEESE TART

This is ideal to make in advance and is a delicious alternative to the usual sandwiches for picnics. Serve with a green salad. Serves 2–4.

6 tomatoes, halved

8oz (225g) readymade puff pastry

2 tbsp pesto sauce

4 sun-dried tomatoes, peeled and finely chopped

4oz (110g) goat cheese, or other cheese if preferred

Salt and pepper to taste

1 tbsp Parmesan shavings

Olive oil

Chopped basil, to garnish

In a medium oven bake the tomatoes in a medium-hot oven until roasted and slightly caramelized (sweet-tasting). Turn up the oven to 425°F (220°C/Gas 7). Roll out the pastry to a 10-inch (25cm) circle and place on an oiled baking sheet. Score a smaller circle 1 inch (2.5cm) inside the pastry circle. Inside the inner circle spread the pesto and arrange the tomato and goat cheese; season and scatter the Parmesan over it. Drizzle with 1tbsp olive oil. Bake the tart for 15 minutes until the pastry is puffed and golden. Garnish with the basil and serve immediately. An alternative is to make this tart with roasted red onions instead of the roasted tomatoes.

NECTARINE AND GINGER FOOL

This is a low-fat dessert that takes only minutes to prepare. It is made in advance and chilled, which means that you can relax over the meal. Serves 2.

7oz (200g) ripe nectarine flesh (about 2 fruit)

1tsp finely chopped crystalized or preserved stem ginger

8oz (225g) low-fat yogurt

1 tbsp syrup from preserved ginger (optional)

1oz (30g) Amaretti cookies, roughly crushed with a rolling pin or pestle

Mix all the ingredients apart from the cookies briefly in a blender for a coarse texture or slightly longer for a smooth texture. Mix in half of the crushed cookies to give it a crunchy texture. Chill in small bowls and sprinkle the remaining crushed cookies on top when ready to serve.

COULIS

A coulis is simply raw fruit that is liquidized and then pressed through a sieve to get rid of any seeds or pulp. It makes a delicious and colorful sauce, and you can add extra ingredients to enhance the flavor if you wish, as in the following ideas:

● Peeled fresh tomatoes with tarragon or basil.
● Raspberries or other berries with a dash of liqueur.
● Kiwi fruit with a little honey if it is sour. The bright green color provides a great contrast to red berry coulis for a colorful presentation.

INDEX

AUTHOR'S ACKNOWLEDGMENTS

To my son Benedict, who unwittingly has shown me that making life simple is an essential prerequisite to sharing laughs and lots of good times. Many thanks to all who have helped me along this road - Cindy, Liz, Georgina, and Carol, and also Laurence, Eden, Brad and Phoebe, Ma, and Marjorie.

The author would like to thank Boots plc for the use of the survey, quoted on page 27: Wellbeing 2002. A study into the nation's wellbeing by Boots plc, United Kingdom. Full survey results are available on www.wellbeing.com.